Who'd A Thought
Deliverance Would Come?

A Stunning Parallel of Mark Chapter 5

Dr. Lucy A. Todd

Dr. Lucy A. Todd

WHO'D A THOUGHT DELIVERANCE WOULD COME?

A Stunning Parallel of Mark Chapter 5

"Inspiring Christian Authors to BE Authors"

Pearly Gates Publishing LLC, Houston, Texas

Who'd A Thought Deliverance Would Come?
A Stunning Parallel of Mark Chapter 5

Copyright © 2017
Dr. Lucy A. Todd

All Rights Reserved.
No portion of this publication may be reproduced, stored in any electronic system, or transmitted in any form or by any means (electronic, mechanical, photocopy, recording, or otherwise) without written permission from the author or publisher. Brief quotations may be used in literary reviews.

ISBN 13: 978-1945117664
ISBN 10: 1945117664
Library of Congress Control Number: 2017933728

Scripture references are taken from The King James, The Message, and Amplified Versions of the Holy Bible. Used with permission from Zondervan Publishing House.

Dr. Lucy A. Todd

DEDICATION

This book is dedicated to my 'Gleesome Threesome': LaDonnica, Tremaine, and Princess. In my darkest moments, all of you have been my glowing flame, my second-wind when I'm beaten down, and my reason to blaze a new trail - consistently forging ahead to destroy the negative heredity while affording the three of you a new inheritance. You are the loves of my life...*my three gifts from God.*

Additionally, I dedicate this book to the younger women and men. My hope is that you will avoid similar addictive pitfalls I've encountered. If you're already caught in those traps of addiction that so easily entangle and intend on never letting go, here is your roadmap to **FREEDOM**! *Deliverance is HERE!*

For all of the women being verbally, mentally, and physically abused...*BEAT DOWN*...**DELIVERANCE** is for you!

For all of the parents believing for their once "cute, adorable, innocent babies" who are now addicted teens or adults to be set free from the grips of addiction...**DELIVERANCE** is for you AND them!

For all of the teens who are being sex-trafficked...**DELIVERANCE** is for you!

For all of the men who are trapped in sexual addictions and pornography...**DELIVERANCE** is for you!

Who'd A Thought Deliverance Would Come?

Penned on the pages of this book, I lay bare my life's story of pain, struggle, love, and redemption with a God-given purpose:

"Guide older women into lives of reverence so they end up as neither gossips nor drunks, but models of goodness. By looking at them, the younger women will know how to love their husbands and children, be virtuous and pure, keep a good house, be good wives. We don't want anyone looking down on God's Message because of their behavior. Also, guide the young men to live disciplined lives."
(Titus 2:3-6)

I promise you, Dear Reader: This book will provide a clear road map to **DELIVERANCE** for you!

Dr. Lucy A. Todd

FROM THE CREATIVE DIRECTOR OF THE BOOK COVER: ARTFUL INSIGHT

While examining fine art in a museum, one will search for meaningful metaphors or symbols in each and every detail. The cover hereon strategically places one woman on the left side of the cover *(we begin reading from left to right)*, who is obviously high on some type of drug that she has intravenously injected into her body - as revealed by the hypodermic needles dropped on the floor near her feet. She is in a seated position, which is indicative of non-movement. She is not moving forward, is in a state of drowsy sleep, has no plans, is not going anywhere with her life, and is possibly wasting away while contemplating her next high. She is seated on a black leather couch, which could be interpreted as staying seated in **darkness**.

30 years ago, the author was in a similar place; however, the author encountered **Jesus Christ** - as portrayed by the woman ascending the stairs in an upward trajectory, fully awake *(we must stay awake)*, having moved away from the seated position, changing her posture and position, while focused on the heavenlies. She is in an upward motion, expanding her vision, using her influence, and taking advantage of *unlimited* opportunities - as portrayed by her business attire and oversized attaché-portfolio case. She has left the Madman (Woman) of the Gadarenes position in Mark Chapter 5 - one of bondage and self-inflicting destructive behavior - and taken on a "never going back" posture and position while in pursuit of **all** that awaits her in her newly-acclaimed deliverance lifestyle.

Who'd A Thought Deliverance Would Come?

PREFACE

When I was just a little girl - around 10 or 11 years old - I "*fell in love*" with a man. However, falling in love didn't mean I would remain faithful to him. Falling in love didn't guarantee I wouldn't one day change partners because I found others more appealing and attractive on life's journey…a reality some of us are incapable of resisting.

In my teen years, I somehow became dissatisfied with "my love". I desired more than what he was offering. I was determined to satisfy what I later determined was an unquenchable desire. I hungered, thirsted, and longed for love - and I sought it out in the most obscure, detestable, and even deplorable places. Some of the younger generation of today (in 2017) would refer to that as being "wretched". It was! It was wretched, indeed! (They actually pronounce it "ratchet", by the way.) Georgia Mass Choir sings the song, "A Wretch Undone!" However, more profoundly, Romans 7:24 speaks on it this way: "*O, wretched man that I am! Who shall deliver me from the body of this death?*"

When you're living in a state of sin and doing things that are not conducive for Godly-living, know that the wages *(or paycheck)* for sin is death. While living a wretched lifestyle, you are spiritually dying. The "real you" is diminishing, and ultimately, the physical body will assume the effects of the starved spirit man - the "real you" on the inside…***your spirit.***

> *WHEN THE SPIRIT IS UNDERNOURISHED, THE BODY SPIRALS DOWNWARD.*

Dr. Lucy A. Todd

W.A.T. = Who'd A Thought?

The year is 2017. Presently, in the United States of America, the use of illegal drugs has become an epidemic. The Surgeon General's Report provided the following statistics:

- 27.1 Million people suffer with Substance Abuse
- 90% are NOT getting treatment
- $400 Billion - Economic Impact / Lost Workplace Productivity

W.A.T.?

Very recently, there was a picture in the news of a police officer checking out a car parked on the side of the road. There was a child in its car seat - approximately one to two years old - very much alive…with both parents in the front seats slumped over from an apparent overdose. Deceased!

W.A.T.?

A few days ago (in January 2017), as I was picking up my dry cleaning, the news on the television inside the business blared: "A 30-year-old decided to sneak away from rehab [he was already receiving treatment]. He drove to purchase drugs and, after injecting heroin into his veins, was making his way back to the rehab when he ran over some children who were playing outside. A nine-year-old was killed." The man will lose YEARS off his life - and the nine-year-old will never know what it's like to be 10 years old.

W.A.T.?

Who'd A Thought Deliverance Would Come?

How about ONE more?

In February 2017, a coroner's morgue was packed full with dead bodies of people who have overdosed. The morgue stated they were running out of room!

W.A.T.?

Heroin, cocaine, meth, and even crack are sabotaging many in professional positions. Respected mothers, fathers, and athletes are falling prey to the grips of the evil talons of addiction that reach deep into the souls of many. Additionally, teens are also being lured and fascinated by the deceitful allure associated with the drug culture.

To be quite honest, today (in 2017) is no different than the 1970s when Marvin Gaye (one of the many celebs known to have dealings in the drug culture) and other recording artists profoundly sang about that questionable era, which included songs like "Flying High in the Friendly Sky". During the 1950s, Billie Holiday's influential jazz career was halted at the young age of 44. She was placed under arrest, while in the hospital for possession of illegal narcotics - and she died there. Whitney Houston had a drug-riddled lifestyle that led to her passing (she was unaware I was her #1 Fan). Last, but not least, the beloved Michael Jackson overdosed and passed away - along with countless other wonderful artists.

In the late 1960s, I experimented with drugs. Needless to say, I got hooked.

Dr. Lucy A. Todd

While reading a family member's journal which was penned during World War II (I should add here...I did so without permission), it was noted there were many warriors entangled in the fantasy and escape of drug abuse between 1939 and 1945. It is my belief there was never an era that was free from drug use...

I cannot say with any certainty that heroin and cocaine were ever the "drug of choice" B.C. (Before Christ), but there sure are mentions in the Holy Bible of a lot of wine drinking and wild partying taking place. In Galatians Chapter Five, "drunkenness" is mentioned as a 'work of the flesh'. In the Old Testament, Noah sure enough had his fill of alcohol after his ride on the Ark for approximately 364 days with all of his relatives! "*And he drank of the wine, and was drunken; and he was uncovered within his tent*" (Genesis 9:21). Can you imagine being locked in a boat with your relatives for any extreme length of time beyond the traditional three-day family reunion?

I submit: The overindulgence and search for the elusive temporary high or escape that is afforded by drug use is an attempt to fill a void, solve a challenge, or replace a missing piece, which is something that should only be administered by the Creator of the human spirit.

When you purchase a vehicle, it comes with a manual. When God created man, He gave him His manual to operate by. That manual is the Bible.

Who'd A Thought Deliverance Would Come?

Seeking to fill a void in one's life with drugs, uncontrollable shopping, sexual perversion, alcoholism, pornography, the corporate chase, another's spouse, gluttony, excessive fitness workouts, ongoing cosmetic transformations, and I'm sure you can name many others…they only create more voids incapable of being fulfilled and generate more problems to address later in life. "*Sin is only pleasurable for a season*" (Hebrews 11:25). However, during that season, it sure was enjoyable - although it only caused more (begets) sin!

Let's refer back to the statement "Sin is only pleasurable for a *SEASON*" (emphasis added). 'Season' is defined as a time characterized by a particular circumstance or feature; a division of the year marked by changes in the weather, ecology, and hours of daylight (Merriam-Webster, 2017). Used in the context above, sin is only pleasurable for a small segment of time. 'Season' is not defined as "permanent". The pleasures enjoyed during sinful activities will be short-lived! Soon, they will no longer bring pleasure. Instead, they will become a demanding monkey on your back, robbing you of any joys you hoped to experience in all of their fullness! They will have you living a lie and being pretentious!

The quest to satisfy the emptiness, seeking love and happiness, and desiring a sense of belonging made my journey extremely bumpy (dare I say "rocky"?) - to describe it in its mildest form. The journey to receive my Doctoral Degree in Business was strenuous. The dissertation process caused undue stress, hair loss, and sleepless nights due to extensive research and a nightly writing routine - oftentimes into the early morning hours…and still had to work full time. All of the dissertation milestones compare lightly to the extensive challenges encountered along the path of drug abuse.

Dr. Lucy A. Todd

Life has its moments - ones that will blindside you, take you by storm, and attempt to completely knock you out of the game with no breath left for a comeback. Whether you are conducting big business in corporate America, orchestrating and holding down all facets of family life (which is an enormous task in and of itself for many - especially single parents), a successful private entrepreneur juggling multiple components of the private business sector, or even one who has to conduct business in an illegal manner, know this:

DELIVERANCE COMES!

Who'd A Thought Deliverance Would Come?

FOREWORD

I would like to say "Thank You" for your unconditional love and sacrifice you've made throughout your life for us (your 3 children). I believe this book will open doors to many more and give encouragement and insight to everyone that has ever had challenges with "any" addictions. Thank you for paving the way.
~ LaDonnica

In life, we cross paths with people we marvel at and without notice they significantly impact our lives in so many positive ways. Dr. Todd is one of those extraordinary people that inspire you to be, do and have more. With emphasis on having more, so that you have more to give. More to give of yourself in every aspect. Dr. Todd is beyond impressive. "Who'd A Thought" she'd write books. I did, but I've also known her all my life, as she is my mother and We Are Todd.
~ Tremaine "MAINE EVENT"

For as long as I can remember, my mother has said: "One of these days, I'm going to write a book! And I'm going to call it *Mark Chapter Five*!" Even though the title has since changed, she finally did it! In fact, when she called me to say she finished her first draft, the reality of her words did not quite sink in until the next day. As a mother, Dr. Todd has taught me to be thoughtful, forever intellectually curious and to love unconditionally. As a woman, she has challenged me to persevere, exceeding my own grand expectations and to remain humble, gracefully. As you read this body of work, her labor of love - decades in the making, I have no doubt that you, too, will come to know and love the woman I'm intensely privileged to call MY Mama, Dr. Lucy Ann Todd.
~Princess
(Publisher's Note: Per the request of the Author, the words penned in the Foreword are unedited and true to the hearts of the individuals who wrote them.)

Dr. Lucy A. Todd

INTRODUCTION

"As Jesus was getting into the boat, the demon-delivered man begged to go along, but He wouldn't let him. Jesus said, "Go home to your own people. Tell them your story - what the Master did, how He had mercy on you.""
(Mark 5:18-19)

WHAT IS DELIVERANCE? What do people mean when they cry out, ***"Deliver me!"*** Webster says 'deliverance' is rescue from moral corruption or evil; salvation - with one of deliverance's definitions being "pronouncement", which is a formal or authoritative statement; an opinion or decision! It all ties in together with my definition:

DELIVERANCE is the act of being set free from any bondage - whether mental, physical, or spiritual - beginning with a clear and decisive desire *AND* declaration of that desired freedom.

> *DELIVERANCE:*
> *RESCUE FROM MORAL*
> *CORRUPTION OR EVIL.*

WHERE DOES DELIVERANCE COME FROM? I say it comes from **GOD**! Genesis 45:7 states, *"And God sent me before you to preserve you a posterity in the Earth, and to save your lives by a great **deliverance**"* (emphasis added). There are many other accounts of God providing deliverance for His people, to include times of war. You are, of course, entitled to your ideas of where deliverance comes from; however, this is **MY** story - and I'm sticking to it!

Who'd A Thought Deliverance Would Come?

WHEN WILL DELIVERANCE COME? I say deliverance comes at **ANY** time! When your heart is ready to get on with the task at hand of being set free, *DELIVERANCE WILL COME!*

"He replied, 'You've been given insight into God's kingdom. You know how it works. Not everybody has this gift, this insight; it hasn't been given to them. Whenever someone has a ready heart for this, the insights and understandings flow freely. But if there is no readiness, any trace of receptivity soon disappears. That's why I tell stories; to create readiness and to nudge the people towards receptive insight. In their present state, they can stare until doomsday and not see it or listen until they're blue in the face and not get it. I don't want Isaiah's forecast repeated all over again:
"Your ears are open, but you don't hear a thing.
Your eyes are awake, but you don't see a thing.
The people are blockheads!
They stick their fingers in their ears so they won't have to listen;
They screw their eyes shut so they won't have to look, so they won't have to deal with me face-to-face and let me heal them"."
(Matthew 13:11-15)

WILL DELIVERANCE COME TO ME? The answer is simple: Only if you believe it will. Do you actually believe deliverance will come for your child who is strung out on crack? If you truly think so, then **STOP** perpetuating the problem and call those things that be not as though they were!

"For as he thinketh in his heart, so is he: Eat and drink, saith he to thee; but his heart is not with thee" (Proverbs 23:7).

Dr. Lucy A. Todd

Believe it or not, there were men in days of old who thought they could build a tower to reach Heaven. Because that was not part of God's plan, He intervened and interrupted them. Why? Because their thoughts (and ours) are capable of manufacturing a lot more than we may credit them for doing. So, let's just say: **Your thoughts are more powerful than you think** (no pun intended)!

Glory to God: I don't look like what I've been through! I had a former life that in *no way* parallels the life I now live. Today, I am a Doctor, Business-Owner, Motivational Speaker, Author, one who enjoys serving others, and a sensitive, caring woman. Many of us have been through some things. Maybe you're not quite ready to share your *"Who'd A Thought?"* moments - and that's perfectly fine. Look how long it has taken me!

Let it be known: I didn't acquire my Doctorate by chance or honorary delivery for great achievements. I **THOUGHT** I could become a Doctor.

Initially, I gained no support from family and friends. My son asked, *"Why don't you just use the degrees you have? Why obtain another one?"* My oldest had no comment, and my youngest daughter was disgruntled with her life's phase at that time. She didn't seem to care one way or the other. Her question was, *"What are you going to do your research on?"* Friends were distant. It was a painfully-emotional time.

My message to you is this: Don't ever allow the way someone else feels about your desired course stop you from jumping in with all that you have. Do the doggone "thang"!

Who'd A Thought Deliverance Would Come?

Sidebar: *My children and grandchildren became my reason for trudging through unchartered waters, in order to give them a legacy and blaze a trail for them to readily follow.*

- Doctors produce Doctors!
- Murderers produce Murderers!
- Addicts produce Addicts!
- Welfare Mamas produce Welfare Mamas!
- Great Chefs produce even Greater Chefs!
- Preachers produce Exemplary Preachers!
- Criminals produce even Worse Criminals!
- University Presidents produce University Presidents! And so on...

Fruit produces after its kind, and I desire a heritage of good fruit! Thus, this journey!

In order to obtain my Doctorate, I studied day and night and operated on two to three hours of sleep each night for several years. One co-worker who had no idea of "my struggle" said to me one morning, "*You look a little rough today.*" If **only** she knew that when you have goals, you do what you've got to do! I was working full time, running businesses full time, going to school full time, researching, writing, praying, crying (often), questioning 'why', studying every waking moment of every day, had no social life at all...and my hair was thinning! There were times I felt I would not make it to the finish line; however, I can truly say I am now the embodiment of God's supernatural grace, love, and (most definitely) **DELIVERANCE**. I am radiating His joy and love to those who will receive.

Dr. Lucy A. Todd

During my graduate studies, professors required more than I thought I could give...many times with them not even knowing what they were requiring. University Administrators were often elusive, Mentors created unnecessary challenges, and cohorts dropped out like fatally-wounded warriors on the battlefield. **BUT** when I felt like giving up, I mustered up the courage to persevere because my youngest child *(who was able to relate to the woes of academia)* impressed upon that one last ounce of fortitude left in me, insisting that I keep going.

"Winners NEVER quit...and Quitters NEVER win!"
~ Vince Lombardi ~

TABLE OF CONTENTS

DEDICATION -- **VI**

FROM THE CREATIVE DIRECTOR OF THE BOOK COVER: ARTFUL INSIGHT ------- **VIII**

PREFACE -- **IX**

FOREWORD -- **XV**

INTRODUCTION -- **XVI**

CHAPTER ONE: MADMAN [WOMAN] OF GADARENES ------------------------------- **1**

CHAPTER TWO: DWELLING IN THE DEAD PLACES --------------------------- **21**

CHAPTER THREE: MEET THE MAN AND DELIVERER --------------------------- **26**

CHAPTER FOUR: CONTAMINATION 101 -- **27**

CHAPTER FIVE: JESUS' MARKETING PLAN --------------------------------- **33**

CHAPTER SIX: DISTRACTION, DISTRACTIONS, AND MORE DISTRACTIONS! ------ **35**

CHAPTER SEVEN: THEY LAUGHED, BUT I LAUGHED BEST! ---------------------- **40**

CHAPTER EIGHT: JUST BE FREE! -- **44**

CHAPTER NINE: BEAUTIFIED AND DIGNIFIED ------------------------------------ **50**

CHAPTER TEN: IT'S TIME TO RENEW YOUR MIND -------------------------------- **64**

CHAPTER ELEVEN: PIE IN THE SKY! --- **68**

CHAPTER TWELVE: BELIEVE ME: BELIEVE! ------------------------------------ **74**

CHAPTER THIRTEEN: GOD-GIVEN CREATIVE ABILITY ---------------------------- **79**

CHAPTER FOURTEEN: I THOUGHT I LACKED WHAT WAS ACROSS THE TRACKS - **82**

CHAPTER FIFTEEN: CHANGE YOUR MIND, CHANGE YOUR WORDS, CHANGE YOUR LIFE! -- **87**

CHAPTER SIXTEEN: HOPE BEYOND HOPE --- 94

CHAPTER SEVENTEEN: IF NOT YOU, THEN WHO? -------------------------------------- 106

CHAPTER EIGHTEEN: WE ARE OUR BROTHER'S KEEPER ------------------------------ 112

CHAPTER NINETEEN: IT'S NOT TOO LATE TO BEGIN ANEW ------------------------- 115

CHAPTER TWENTY: LEARN TO DREAM BIGGER! -- 123

CHAPTER TWENTY-ONE: FORGIVENESS...IT'S FOR YOU! ---------------------------- 130

CHAPTER TWENTY-TWO: HOW DOES DELIVERANCE COME? ------------------------ 139

CHAPTER TWENTY-THREE: HOW TO STAY IN THE DELIVERANCE-ZONE --------- 141

CHAPTER TWENTY-FOUR: IT'S TIME TO SILENCE THOSE NEGATIVE VOICES ---- 144

CHAPTER TWENTY-FIVE: PROMPTING OF THE SPIRIT -------------------------------- 150

CHAPTER TWENTY-SIX: QUIET TIME: TIME TO MEDITATE --------------------------- 154

CHAPTER TWENTY-SEVEN: THE HARVEST IS ALWAYS GREATER THAN THE SEED
--- 158

CONCLUSION --- 161

DELIVERANCE CONFESSIONS & AFFIRMATIONS --------------------------------------- 167

MY ANCHOR SCRIPTURE --- 172

ABOUT THE AUTHOR-- 173

BIBLIOGRAPHY-- 175

CHAPTER ONE
MadMan (Woman) of Gadarenes

"They arrived on the other side of the sea in the country of the Gadarenes. As Jesus got out of the boat, a madman from the cemetery came up to Him. He lived there among the tombs and graves. No one could restrain him – he couldn't be chained, couldn't be tied down. He had been tied up many times with chains and ropes, but he broke the chains, snapped the ropes. No one was strong enough to tame him. Night and day, he roamed through the graves and the hills, screaming out and slashing himself with sharp stones."
(Mark 5:1-5)

Why is the man with the unclean spirit - the Madman...demoniac - cutting himself in the graveyard among the tombs? Was he not taught to appreciate the gift of life and to love himself as God does? What was wrong with the Madman of Gadarenes?

CRAZY. WILD. LOST...kind of like the Madman of Gadarenes! How did that happen to **me**? How did I find myself destroying my body with drugs by injecting narcotics into my veins? How did my husband and I end up participating in activities that dated back to biblical times? Why would anyone try to destroy themselves with food, drugs, alcohol, extortion, pornography, illicit sex, deceit, excessive body enhancements, working excessively, uncontrollable addictive shopping, etc.?

The Word of God clearly states, *"...there is nothing new under the sun"* (Ecclesiastes 1:9). I can guarantee you: For **every** single thing going on in your life - both the good and the bad - it's in the Bible!

Come... Go with me...

MadMan [Woman] of Gadarenes

How Did I Get Caught Up (a.k.a. 'Yoked Up')?

Many may have never experienced life on a farm; thus, I will paint a picture of "yoked up" for you.

During my junior high years, integration took place in the school systems. There was a great deal of fear on both sides of the fence. In our school, the Black students had fear because we were outnumbered. The White students had fear because of the stigma associated with Blacks. *I can't forget to mention the predominantly White staff and faculty also shared in the fear of the unknown.*

One day, one of my friends from the 'rough side of the tracks' gave me his jacket and asked me to place it in my locker. I immediately noticed his jacket was quite heavy. That's when he informed me it had a gun inside. I wanted to appear to be "cool", so I said, "*Sure. You can put it in my locker.*" At the time, we were both in 7th Grade. Never in my life had I held a gun until I entered junior high. Thank **GOD** there were no uprisings and no occasion was presented that would have prompted the use of firearms. **Where did he obtain a weapon from anyway?**

We transitioned through those times with only a few bumps along the way. One incident I clearly recall involved my reactionary response to a White male classmate walking behind me as we changed classes. I overheard him referencing one of my fellow Black students with the 'N word'! At the time, I was walking up the steps, dropped my books, turned around, belted him in his mouth, and **DARED** him to say it again. He turned beet red in his lettered jacket!

Where did he learn such language? Where did my reaction stem from?

Who'd A Thought Deliverance Would Come?

I was raised in a great home. My parents had only **ONE** loud disagreement I can recall...

I was rehearsing piano lessons at a neighboring church. My aunt (who was visiting during the Summer and happens to be one year younger than me) ran into the church and said, "Come quickly! Arrie and Sammie are arguing!" That was it. An argument. My parents were not violent in any way, shape, or form. I, however, engaged in little fights with my friends - but nothing major.

Back to the incident with the White male student in the hallway.

That was one of the occasions wherein an action bypassed my head and was acted upon without thought. Of course, we later went to the principal's office and were given very long lectures, but neither of us went to jail nor were our parents called. Neither of us lost time learning because of in or out of school detention and we worked through our differences. Apologies were made and we continued on with our studies.

Handling disagreements in schools today are a lot different...

Smoking Pot in High School

During this era, junior high consisted of 7th, 8th, and 9th grades; high school consisted of 10th, 11th, and 12th. I made the necessary adjustments to integration and my senior high years went very well. I crossed the color lines and began having White friends. My Black friends did not like the way I was able to interact with the White students and began to call me "Oreo". That was okay; "Oreo" was learning how to smoke cigarettes in the bathroom with my White friends...which later escalated to marijuana.

MadMan [Woman] of Gadarenes

Every morning, "Oreo" was feeling very good about going to school because my new friends and I would meet up and ride to school together. We would get so high on the way and enjoy laughing at those who did not understand our common bond. My new friends and I decided to experiment with a prescription drug, and we used it intravenously.

How many of you know that if you let the devil ride, he's going to want to drive?

My parents worked most of the time, so there was no one around to question or counsel me about my friends, my comings, nor my goings. My parents gave me **everything** I wanted...*except themselves*. I really wanted them to be there for my acting performances, my drill team skillful executions, clarinet solos, choir performances, on-point articulate Easter and Christmas speeches, and singing at the Mayor's Induction Ceremony - but they were **working**. Working (I'm sure) to ensure I had nice things... They gave me a car on my 15th birthday, and that was the beginning of many sorrows - many of which I will share along this discourse.

After having to wait several months for graduation day because I had completed all of my studies ahead of schedule, I finally graduated from high school. Although I got high, I excelled in my studies because my dad stressed the importance of a quality education.

ALL junkies are not unlearned! They're just locked in a habitual cycle that does not allow exit strategies easily...if at all.

Who'd A Thought Deliverance Would Come?

The day after high school graduation, I moved to New York. New York , New York; a city so nice, they had to name it twice (a song by Gerard Kenny made in 1978)! I wanted to see the big city and possibly work there. I lived with my brother and his family outside of the city in Mount Vernon and was introduced to heroin after bragging to my brother about my prescription drug use. He was living very well-off, being the best body shop man in New York. He was extremely gifted when it came to making cars look like they had never been impacted by an accident. He was exceptional in his craft and, as a result, lived the good life. The introduction to heroin was quite a drastic transition from prescription drugs. However, I enjoyed *(what was termed back then)* the 'White Horse in the Blue Tape'. The 'White Horse' soon became a big, black **monkey** on my back and I became the Lady Who Sang the Blues!

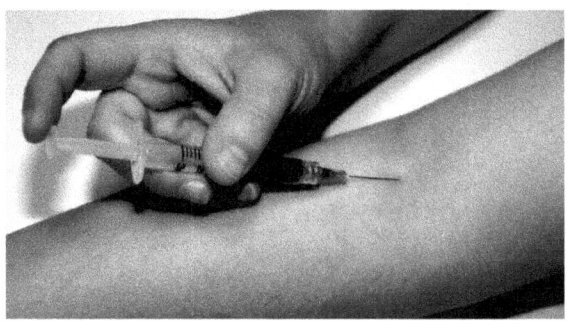

Heroin plays for keeps! It shows you some enjoyment for a *very* short time. Afterwards, it puts its talons in you so deep in hopes of **destroying** your very life.

Heroin is an opiate. It causes a sense of relaxation, almost into a state of sleep. You feel as if you have a beautiful, dark life with an extreme state of peace, but when that addiction manifests and you find a 500-pound **gorilla** on your back, you're in serious trouble. Like any pet or animal, it wants to be fed regularly. It demands being fed on a daily basis - often several times a day. If you don't have money to feed your habit, means must be provided - whether through your willingness to steal, rob, forge checks, sell drugs, sell your body…and your soul. Many people attempt to sell the drugs to other addicts to ensure their personal habits are satisfied.

BUT…

How can you sell something you enjoy *AND* are in desperate need of? That's like owning a bakery, loving baked goods beyond anything in this world, and exercising no restraints on your intake of pastries, cakes, pies, rolls, breads, and donuts daily. Soon, there is no profit because the owner has personally consumed it all!

Escalation to Heroin and Cocaine

Having no job and no one to pay for a free "get high ride" every day, I had to find a means to support my gorilla habit: heroin.

Believe me when I say: **He was very expensive!**

Who'd A Thought Deliverance Would Come?

In order to maintain, I began shopping with a guy we called "Alexander Monday". He was a professional thief...and I needed help generating income. He did all of the "shopping/shoplifting", and I was the imposter "wife/decoy". We made **hundreds** of dollars a day - which was quite a bit of cash 35-40 years ago. We dressed exceptionally well (which was easy to do because of our [shoplifting] careers). We were feeling good **EVERY** day and had *more* than enough monies to purchase our drugs of choice. However, all good things must come to an end (or so they say) - and bad things, too! **THANK GOD!**

Attracting More of the Same

Some say, "Opposites attract". I, however, think *like-spirits* attract. I have gone from the East coast to the West coast and didn't know **anyone** in the drug scene on the West coast, yet I was always able to find those like-minded spirits who enjoyed getting high!

"Back then", during my years of bondage, we had NO internet, NO cell phones, and NO GPS. There's only one way to explain how the connections with other addicts were successful from coast to coast...being led by evil spirits.

> *WE CONTINUE THE SAME HABITS UNTIL WE REPLACE THOSE OLD THOUGHTS AND HABITS WITH NEW ONES.*

In order to do away with a negative thought, you must consciously replace it with a positive thought - preferably a scripture that you've chosen to meditate on all throughout any given day.

MadMan [Woman] of Gadarenes

I had not renewed my mind. I continued to focus all of my thinking on men who were good-looking and liked to party…and I found them! I enjoyed getting high and found others who enjoyed doing the same.

Strange thing: They always thought I was an undercover cop because they said I didn't "fit in". I'd ask, "*Why so?*" and would **proudly** display my needle tracks. The response was often, "*It is just something about you. You should not be doing this.*"

WOW! Just…WOW!

All the while, I kept thinking the same old low-down, dirty, get high, have a good time, party-hardy, loosey booty thoughts - and I kept attracting more of the same.

Nothing changes until you change your thoughts. **NOTHING!** Start thinking success and abundant life, and you will create that. Remember: "*As a man thinketh in his heart, so is he*" (Proverbs 23:7). You lay down with dogs, you get up with fleas! *Evil communications corrupt good manners* (1 Corinthians 15:33), *but iron sharpens iron* (Proverbs 27:17).

Who'd A Thought Deliverance Would Come?

Hang around people who are doing great things, and your desires will change. If friends or co-workers are talking filth and you know you were not raised in an environment that allowed filth to be spoken, then remove yourself. What you will find is that over time, if you don't change your environment, you will become numb to the fact that it is filth and you will think it's okay for people to talk like that in your presence. *IT IS NOT OKAY!*

UNCLEAN: So Dirty Inside, I STANK on the Outside

My parents always had very nice homes for our family to live in. However, I had begun to hang around people who were not of my upbringing or Christian beliefs. Yes: I was raised on a better side of the tracks than those I had chosen to associate with! I was thinking their thoughts and acting with their actions. Environments are important for desired growth. Those new associates *(note I did **NOT** say 'friends')* operated totally contrary to what had been instilled in me by my parents and Sunday School teachers. *If you think nasty thoughts, you will do nasty things and begin to emit negative, nasty odors.* It is my belief that nasty, evil spirits carry with them foul odors. I picked up spirits that were not of God - and they smelled rotten!

One day, my dad gave me a ride home from work because I had car trouble. He was half drunk when he picked me up and had the nerve to tell **ME** I stank! I will never forget that. I didn't have an odor coming from my underarms. Neither did I smell of any physical odor; however, he may have been trying to tell me in his own way that I had changed…and he was displeased.

That brings about another point.

MadMan [Woman] of Gadarenes

Many times (in my ethnic background), parents did not do a good job of communicating with their children. Still today, many parents expect the schools and churches to train their children. The school and church are **SUPPLEMENTS**. The educational responsibility begins in the home with the parental figures.

My dad was a *very* intelligent man. I'm certain he could have found a better way to say *"...you stank..."* How about, *"The lifestyle you are living and the friends you are keeping are not conducive for your life's goals"*? That would have resonated with me much better than **"...you stank..."** OR, better still, *"I see you're heading down a path that may not get you to where you'd like to end up. Can we talk about it?"* OR, even **BETTER** than that, *"**Let's go to God in prayer and ask for guidance regarding what I see you're dealing with and ask for help in time of need.**"* Did dad do **ANY** of that? **NO!**

Smoking, Drinking, Partying...and Going to Church!

I **REALLY** enjoyed the partying that took place on the "other side" of the tracks. You see, I grew up on the conservative, elite side of town where the teachers and other professionals were always watching the "smart, little girl who was destined to become someone great". When I learned what was across those tracks, I was totally fascinated.

Night clubs.
Storefront grocers.
Pool halls.
Small business owners.
The "numbers" (gambling) man.
Gamblers.
Illegal liquor sales on Sundays *(during the 1970s through the 1990s, liquor was not sold on Sundays)*.
AND...DRUGS, DRUGS, DRUGS!

Who'd A Thought Deliverance Would Come?

I thoroughly enjoyed the party scene. The Word of God says that sin is pleasurable. I say 'AMEN' to that! Moses enjoyed the pleasures of sin for a season. Sin is attractive, pleasurable, intriguing, and fascinating - especially when you've only known your side of town all of your life and haven't gone anywhere but to the beach and back to your hometown in the country.

God created variety, and it is a parent's responsibility to expose their children to different facets of life.

I recently read a meme (a quote on social media embedded in a picture or graphic design) that stated, "*The world is a book, and those who do not travel read only a page*" (Saint Augustine). If not through world travels and multiple activities, at least afford your children the luxury of traveling and exploring through books. In his book, *Act Like a Success, Think Like a Success*, Steve Harvey said that his mom would bring home magazines and help him dream of other countries. She never had the opportunity to take him to those places; however, she took the time to **expose** him to far-off places. He has since frequented those places of which he used to dream.

> *THE WORLD IS A BOOK, AND THOSE WHO DO NOT TRAVEL READ ONLY A PAGE.*

It is necessary to shape children's minds and worlds while they are young. I believe if my parents had exposed me to more opportunities, they would have created a stronger desire in me to succeed. I cannot say for *certain*, but I like to believe I might have chosen a different path than the one I ultimately chose. However, I am thankful I took that path because I can share with you how to avoid those pitfalls and (hopefully) show you how to not take that path. As well, if you are already on that path or know someone who is, this book will show you how to get on the path to the good life because **DELIVERANCE** does come!

I used to smoke two packs of cigarettes a day. I even developed "Smoker's Cough"! Every other breath I took, I coughed. It was **ugly**. After about 20 years of smoking, I realized it was debilitating.

One day (remember always: **WHEN YOU'RE READY, DELIVERANCE IS THERE!**), I made up my mind that although I "enjoyed" smoking, I would lay it to rest. I told God I was drawing a line in the sand - and I literally did just that. I then stepped across that line and I've never smoked another cigarette *(or anything else, for that matter)* since that day! I said, *"God, if you are real, I know that cigs are not good for me. My son has asthma and I don't need to be smoking around him. I believe you are THE DELIVERER!"*

Who'd A Thought Deliverance Would Come?

Guess what happened? **NO** withdrawals. **NO** more hacking cough. **NO** more desire. **NO** more *BONDAGE*! **THAT** is how powerful our God is! He did it for me, and He will do it for *YOU*!

> *"GOD IS NO RESPECTER OF PERSONS."*
> *ACTS 10:34*

Today, I love and enjoy every day of my life. I am happy and enjoy sharing the joy I have with others. I work to have constant fellowship with the Lord as I come and go. Talking to myself and enjoying the internal dialogue helps me deal with all of the exterior drama. Internal dialogue is important because of all we have bombarding our minds today. Internal dialogue is my **real self** (my spirit woman) talking to God. He moved inside of me when I invited Jesus to move in. He will keep you happy. He has a sense of humor, and I find myself thanking Him often for where He has delivered me from. A grateful heart is a happy heart! I have **SO** much to be grateful for!

One of the Associate Pastors at my church once made a comment that I am always smiling. He went on to say that I must have had some dental work done recently and simply wanted to show it off. I just smiled because *everyone* doesn't know what the Lord has delivered me from. They don't know how grateful, free, and **genuinely** happy I am - so I let them assume I smile because of dental work!

In life, you will find that everyone has their own opinion. They are entitled to it and you have no right to impose your opinion upon them. Just be **HAPPY**! *"Sufficient for the day is the evil thereof, so don't choose to have unnecessary battles"* (Matthew 6:34).

We Hear Negative Reports About Priests in the Catholic Church, but What About the Methodist and Baptist Churches?

Many times, I've seen on the news stories about Catholic Priests molesting boys; however, I heard very little about the Methodist and Baptist Pastors who worked overtime to get into my pants as I was coming out of a lifestyle of sin and shame. I was thinking that running **to** God was the way to go! Those are things many people opt to not talk about because of guilt and shame. I know. It happened to me. *I wonder how many more attractive young ladies desiring to surrender their lives to the Lord with the help of the church found themselves being pushed back into a dark hole?*

I tell my children that Pastors and Priests are mankind. We should respect everyone; however, all of us are subject to the temptations of the enemy and can fall if we are not mindful. Just like many of the little boys who were affronted by the Priests they trusted, I, too, was innocent and taken advantage of by men of God who I thought had my best interests at heart. The Word tells us that in the last days, if it were possible, the very elect could be deceived (Matthew 24:24).

Who'd A Thought Deliverance Would Come?

Another thing (while we're here discussing mankind being deceived): Don't be deceived into thinking your uncle, son, or cousin would **never** sexually touch your daughter or son. A perverted, unrenewed mind and a hardened, erect penis knows no relatives and will listen very intently to the desires of the erection - as opposed to reason. **PLEASE**: Utilize good judgment regarding whom you will allow your children to be with privately.

If you are in that situation right now…if you are a victim of the unrenewed mind, ask God to lead you to a church where He would have you to go, and He will. There are genuine Pastors throughout the world who will build you up in the Word of God. No one can ever make you feel bad about yourself again. When **GOD** forgives you, please work on forgiving **yourself** and letting go of past thoughts of illicit behaviors (Philippians 3:13-14). Your spirit man gets born again when Jesus moves in; however, your body and soul (which is your mind, will, and emotions) may take a little longer to catch up with your spirit. Still, continue to go to church. Read your Bible and other inspirational literature. Before you know it, your human being will become subject to your spirit-being and you will walk in the newness of life! It is a process. Your hands do not look new, and neither do your feet! Your constant feeding of the Word of God, Psalms, and hymns will make your real inner-man grow strong. The healthy reflection from the inside will permeate your physical being. You can change your exterior with your interior upgrades.

> *"AS A MAN THINKETH IN HIS HEART, SO IS HE…"*
> *PROVERBS 23:7*

MadMan [Woman] of Gadarenes

I was so hungry for God and sought Him in every way: books, Christian TV, church, and home Bible studies. There was this one Bible study I attended, and I grew by leaps and bounds there. We would watch videos and listen to recorded messages by R.W. Schambach, Kathryn Kuhlman videos, Kenneth Copeland, Novell Hayes, Oral Roberts Tent Meetings, John Osteen meetings, T.L. Osborne sermons, Dr. Fred Price, and others who had materials we could obtain to use during home meetings. We would pray and believe God - and get results! Kenneth Hagin came to a neighboring town, and I drove for hours to see him as well. I also attended storefront churches. Wherever I thought the power of God was, my children and I were there!

God protected me from bad teachings, too. He knew I was coming for Him…**HARD**. Not only did I receive Jesus as my Lord and Savior; I also received the Gift of the Holy Spirit with the evidence of speaking in tongues. That Gift affords you the opportunity to pray directly to God without interference. You pray the perfect prayer, give perfect thanksgiving, and perfect praise - all at the same time! Bet you can't touch that! ☺

God is praying through you exactly what you need to pray for regarding multiple situations. Some are dealing with you and yours. Others speak to and about people you don't even know. Don't just be okay with getting saved. Take **ALL** that God is giving. Get the baptism of the Holy Spirit! You will never be the same again. After receiving the Gift of Jesus and saying "no" to the Gift of the Holy Spirit of God and a supernatural prayer language is the same as leaving gifts under the Christmas tree and saying, "I will only take one".

I am not rejecting **ANYTHING** God has for me! I'm taking it **ALL**!

Who'd A Thought Deliverance Would Come?

Sodom and Gomorrah: Picking Up All KINDS of Spirits

The devil is crazy and will suggest to you some weird things for you to do. When you're under the influence of dangerous narcotics or too much alcohol, you may do some super-dumb things and, when you're sober, you find yourself asking, "*DID I DO THAT?*" (**IF** you can even recall...)

Sexual perversion while under the influence is commonplace. "Swinging" (the act of exchanging sexual partners; yes, even husbands and wives) has become acceptable in today's society. People openly discuss their trysts in the sack with others' spouses and multiple partners, and it is disheartening.

W.A.T.?

The enemy delivers packages in the form of thoughts, well-dressed men and women, a good business deal, a "free" high that won't remain free for long, flattering comments, a pair of Louboutins or a Gucci dress on sale that you REALLY can't afford either way, food that is unhealthy (see Proverbs 23:3), and a plethora of other vices. **DID YOU KNOW?** You do not have to sign for those packages! Just because it's delivered to your thought-life does **NOT** mean you have to sign for it! Mark it undeliverable and ***RETURN TO SENDER***!

"After all, we don't want to unwittingly give Satan an opening for yet more mischief - we're not oblivious to his sly ways!"
(2 Corinthians 2:11)

MadMan [Woman] of Gadarenes

The Bible talks about how sexual sins and wild partying are sins against the body. When you have sex with multiple partners, you pick up multiple spirits. So, when you leave an orgy (for example), you don't leave the same way you came. You have some "guests" riding shotgun. You have picked up others' spirits - ones that are unseen - and they sometimes influence you to act in a manner that is distasteful. You wonder, *"Where is this behavior coming from?"* If you didn't know before, **NOW YOU KNOW!**

"There's more to sex than mere skin to skin. Sex is as much spiritual mystery as physical fact. As written in Scripture, "The two become one." Since we want to become spiritually one with the Master, we must not pursue the kind of sex that avoids commitment and intimacy, leaving us more lonely than ever - the kind of sex that can never "become one". There is a sense in which sexual sins are different from all others. In sexual sin, we violate the sacredness of our own bodies, these bodies that were made for God-given and God-modeled love, for "becoming one" with another. Or didn't you realize that your body is a sacred place, the place of the Holy Spirit? Don't you see that you can't live however you please, squandering what God paid such a high price for? The physical part of you is not some piece of property belonging to the spiritual part of you.
God owns the whole works.
So let people see God in and through your body."
(1 Corinthians 6:16-20)

Who'd A Thought Deliverance Would Come?

"Yoked Up" Concluded...

Did I go through all that I did **AND** arrive where I am today by chance? OR was it all part of 'THE PLAN'?

I consider the multiple negative encounters I endured in my life and often wonder, *"Where did I go wrong? How did I get off course? Did I **REALLY** live through all of that?"*

I recall Moses telling Pharaoh to let God's people go. The Bible says that **GOD** (the One who told Moses to go tell Pharaoh to let His people go) was the **SAME GOD** who hardened Pharaoh's heart (see Exodus 7:3)!

I must question: Did I go through all of that and rebel against what I knew I should do (as opposed to what I wanted to do)? If I did, did I go through all of that for **YOU** so I could share my testimony to encourage you? God **DELIVERED** me! Rest assured: *SURELY*, He will do the same for you or your loved one!

Whatever the dependence, there is DELIVERANCE!

Now that you have a picture of being 'yoked up', allow me to share Webster's definition of 'yoke': "A device for joining together a pair of draft animals, especially oxen, usually consisting of a crosspiece with two bow-shaped pieces, each enclosing the head of an animal; something that couples or binds together; a bond or tie."

MY definition of 'yoke' is this:

*Being connected (by whatever means) to something that restricts, dominates, and controls you -
leaving no room nor ability to break free!*

CLINK! CLINK! LOCK DOWN!

CHAPTER TWO
Dwelling in the Dead Places

Where is Gadarenes?

Origen (3rd Century) identifies 'Gergesa' as "an ancient city" in the vicinity of the Sea of Tiberias - the site of the miracle of the swine. Sea of Tiberias is also the name used for the Sea of Galilee in 2nd Century rabbinic literature; hence, Origen has preserved historically-reliable details.

The miracle of the swine took place during Jesus' visit to the land of the Gadarenes…the same place the Madman of the tombs was found hanging out when he finally received his deliverance from **ALL** that held him captive.

DEAD PLACE: The Dirty Hotel Rooms

I was sick and tired and tired and sick of the filthy areas I found myself in, but never quite sick enough to leave. I once asked God (while climbing the stairs to a shooting gallery - a place where drug addicts convene for a small fee to inject drugs into their veins while "supposedly" being safe from the law), **"When are you going to deliver me from this life?"** I abhorred my lifestyle, but also enjoyed the escape afforded by the drugs.

That was very similar to what Paul penned: "*For that which I do I allow not: for what I would, that do I not; but what I hate, that do I*" (Romans 7:15).

> *I'VE SPENT A LONG TIME IN SIN'S PRISON. WHAT I DON'T UNDERSTAND ABOUT MYSELF IS THAT I DECIDE ONE WAY, BUT THEN I ACT ANOTHER - DOING THINGS I ABSOLUTELY DESPISE.*

DEAD PLACE: The Filthy Night Clubs

Another dead place: those filthy night clubs. I'm not talking about just physically filthy *(which they were)*. I'm **also** referring to the things that went on in them being filthy as well. Filthy spirits have **FUN** through people in those places. Oh, how I wanted to *STOP* wandering around in the cemetery of sin, failure, and "jones-ing" (sickness from addiction). I needed to step into the resurrection life afforded by Christ, but no one was there to show me how to get out!

I'm writing my testimony to help **YOU** get out and into your best life ever - in Christ!

What I'm about to say is **VERY** important: *Don't ever be ashamed of the pit God dug you out of.* We've all been delivered from the down and dirty sinful nature (see Romans 5:4).

There is no "little sin" and no "big sin". **SIN IS SIN!** Don't let people look down on you because you have a mote [speck] in your eye and they have a **LOG** in theirs!

Who'd A Thought Deliverance Would Come?

DEAD PLACE: The Dirty Mind

The dirty mind of a sinful man is infiltrated by the one controlling the mind...the devil himself.

DEAD PLACE: Across the Track

Across the track... That life was **so** engaging and exciting for me as a girl from the 'good side' of town. I was captivated!

DEAD PLACE: Listening to Death Lyrics

Music, just as words and thoughts can create life or death. During the dark period of my life, I listened to Hard Rock music and countless other artists who were not creating wholesome music. Many of those same artists died from overdoses or committed suicide.

If you're listening to music that arouses sexual desires, then guess what? You're going to want to satisfy those feelings! Prayerfully, you're married and mature enough to stick with one partner when enjoying those sounds...

DEAD PLACE: Smoking Rooms

Today, smoking rooms are now called 'Hookahs'. Back in the 60s and 70s, they were the rooms in the back of lounges or restaurants where folks relaxed, smoked marijuana, and consumed other drugs...wayyy in the back of the club.

There are so many similarities I see today that were prevalent in yesteryears.

Same devil. Different approach

Dwelling in the Dead Places

Dr. Caroline Leaf is a powerful neuroscientist and author of *Think and Eat Yourself Smart*. Dr. Leaf has confirmed my thoughts on so many levels regarding words, thoughts, and music - as well as food. She explains how our thoughts and words grow trees in our brains. If you're focused on the negative deadly lyrics, then music will grow death, just as unhealthy food grows death in the physical body. Many of the songs I listened to spoke to the drug culture, wars, division in our country, and sexual satisfaction - quite similar to what's happening today. You really are what you eat, listen to, and speak!

Dr. Leaf teaches how to uproot the negative trees in the brain with this simple plan: **Replace them with healthy trees, all by thinking and speaking healthy thoughts.**

God really knew what He meant when He said, "*As a man thinketh in his heart, so is he*" (Proverbs 23:7).

Dr. Leaf states, "*What you think affects what you eat, and what you eat affects what you think.*" We must think **and** eat better. Our elders didn't run by fast food restaurants for dinner. Neither did they have the TV, radio, internet, and smartphones to constantly invade their space and minds with every facet of advertising. Marketing is coming at us from every angle at 100 miles per hour. Controlling what you allow into your eyes, ears, and mouth is a 24/7 job. If someone could invent filters and program them to allow only good things to enter our minds, bodies, and spirits, life would be *heavenly*! Fortunately, that is something we are capable of doing for ourselves.

"Keep thy heart with all diligence, for out of it are the issues of life."
Proverbs 4:23

Who'd A Thought Deliverance Would Come?

Get free from distractions and temptations. **FOCUS!** You are a **FAITH FORCE!**

> *THOSE TRAPPED IN ADDICTIONS ARE ON AUTO-PILOT...OF SELF-DESTRUCTION.*

Replace seeking drugs and other addictive behaviors with seeking *JESUS*! Do it like a maniac...frantically so!

CHAPTER THREE
Meet THE MAN and DELIVERER

"When he saw Jesus a long way off, he ran and bowed in worship before Him..."
Mark 5:6

In case you don't know, God is **ALWAYS** there - waiting for you with open arms! The world tried to steal you away from God, but God is married to the backslider. He has promised us a supply of the Sprit, the help we need if we allow God to help us. The more we try to get away from Him, the more He bestows His love upon us. That's called *GRACE*!

Take note of the story of the wandering Israelites in Joshua Chapter Five. God's love was put to the **TEST** with those jokers!

In Luke 11:14, Jesus cast out a demon from a man who could not speak. When the demon was cast out, the man began to speak. Speaking is vitally important to your deliverance! What you say out of your mouth is vitally important to your total well-being and success! You don't want to leave the space the demon was cast out of vacant, either. **IMMEDIATELY** ask God to fill your temple with His Spirit. Why do I instruct you to do that? Let's see what the Scripture has to say! *"When an evil spirit leaves a person, it goes into the desert, searching for rest. But when it finds none, it says, "I will return to the person I came from."* (Luke 11:24)

So, the evicted demon spirit returns to its former Holy Spirit-lacking host. What does it do? It has found seven other spirits - more evil than itself - and reenters the person to set up camp, making life worse off than before! Don't leave that space vacant! **Ask God to fill you UP!**

CHAPTER FOUR
Contamination 101

I believe one of the main reasons Satan wants to contaminate your soul is to destroy your purpose. If he can just keep you from fulfilling God's will for your life, he's been successful. He tries to contaminate your soul through the eyes, ears, and mouth. Don't allow the enemy to invade your soul (mind, will, and emotions)!

Look at bad things, and he'll make those things desirous to you.
Listen to bad things, and he'll make them take root inside of you.
Speak bad things, and he'll have them manifest inside **AND** outside of you.

#####

CONTAMINANT: Smoking

I used to think cigarette commercials were the coolest thing. To top it off, both of my parents smoked. I hated cigarette smoke when I was a child. Whenever we would ride in the car together as a family, I would always complain about the smoke. I bet you can't believe it, but I made a pronouncement then: **I WILL NEVER SMOKE CIGARETTES!** Oops. I smoked! ☺ I sure did! In the bathrooms at school, we smoked cigarettes and Mary Jane (slang for marijuana). I did not smoke at home, however. I was attempting to maintain the image my parents had of their lovely "do-no-wrong' daughter, Lucy.

One morning, I walked into the kitchen. My parents were already there having breakfast. I said, "*Good morning!*", and my mom replied, "*Is that a pack of cigarettes in your robe pocket?*" There was no hiding it. I said, "*Yes, it is.*"

That was **IT.** No one said *ANYTHING* else to me about it. It felt so strange to not receive a lecture! *How **could** they lecture me while actively engaged in the act of smoking themselves?* Furthermore, how could I stand a chance of avoiding that spirit of nicotine/smoking when it was prevalent all of my life in close proximity? Really... **What could they have said?** They both smoked and were setting the examples for me to follow.

Note to parents: Your actions speak a *LOT* louder than your words.

Being honest here: I actually enjoyed smoking. A good menthol cigarette after a nice meal or with a drink was absolutely wonderful! I felt elegant when I smoked. I now know it was the devil tricking me with those feelings of euphoria and grandeur.

One of my younger cousins said she wanted to learn how to smoke just so she could hold her cigarette like I held mine. How whack was **that?** It was the enemy reinforcing the thoughts I had of being "all that and a bag of chips" when I smoked.

Somebody PLEASE tell me: What looks good about that image?

Who'd A Thought Deliverance Would Come?

As mentioned previously, I smoked for over 20 years. The habit grew to a two-pack-a-day habit. That cigarette cough? It was **ROUGH**. I guess my lungs were contaminated with all the smoke and charcoal inhaled. I actually told God I enjoyed smoking (there's nothing like being honest with **HIM**), but I knew it was not good for my health. I asked Him to deliver me - and He did! Praise God for deliverance! God is so good to me! **NO MORE SMOKING! NO MORE COUGHING!**

God is a very present help in the time of trouble. He never leaves me nor forsakes me. He is a Paraclete (Advocate, Intercessor, and Holy Spirit), having already gone before me and prepared the way. Then, He came back, got me, and took me along the way! He's good like that! You really should get to know Him for yourself. What a *FRIEND* we have in Jesus!

CONTAMINANT: Drinking Alcohol

Not only did I smoke; I had a serious drinking problem as well. My family entertained their friends often. When they did, there was alcohol present at the parties. Every day, my dad drank and kept several fifths of liquor in the kitchen cabinet. He got drunk almost every day of his adult life until he decided to quit. He did well for a year or two, then returned to his addiction - like many of us do when we try to overcome any type of addiction in our own strength.

> *"As a dog returneth to his vomit, so a fool returneth to his folly."*
> Proverbs 26:11

Contamination 101

How could I escape being an alcoholic when it was so prevalent in my life from as far back as I can remember? I remember I used to drink my dad's liquor and then fill the bottle up with water. I was a bad girl! My friends and I would party-hardy, loosey-booty - and my dad would never say a thing about it. He would simply get into his nice car and drive to the plaza that had a liquor store to purchase *more liquor!* My dad actually had a credit account at the liquor store! It was not a liquor store in the "hood", either. It was a prominent business in a shopping plaza owned by Caucasians! I went with him on several occasions because I enjoyed riding along. He must have had **GOOD** credit, by the way, because he always got what he wanted.

Alcohol is a legal drug. It alters your consciousness. It kills people on the highway. It causes birth defects. It breaks up happy homes. It can cause you to do and say things you wouldn't when sober. It makes you ask everybody, *"What did I do last night while we were out together?"*

It is my belief that everything has purpose and that wine and other alcoholic beverages were used in ancient days, as well as today for health reasons and celebratory occasions. However, as with food, all must be executed in the confines of moderation. Any and everything can become harmful when allowed to exceed established boundaries. I don't judge others because we are all at different levels of wisdom and growth.

Who'd A Thought Deliverance Would Come?

CONTAMINANT: Intravenous Injections

Alcohol wasn't enough. I heard someone once say you shouldn't give the devil a ride because he'll want to drive. Well, once I gave him access with the cigarettes, Mary Jane, and alcohol, he wanted to take the wheel! He made certain I was introduced to LSD, Acid, Paregoric, Heroin, AND Cocaine. He brought **ALL** of his buddies over to hang out and take turns at the wheel! Guess what I did? I took a seat in the back and allowed him to drive. For 20 years, he tried to drive me straight to Hell, **BUT GOD!**

God, in His grace, saw fit to save me! He will *ALWAYS* provide a way of escape if you want one!

"There hath no temptation taken you but such as is common to man: but God is faithful, who will not suffer you to be tempted above that ye are able; but will with the temptation also make a way to escape, that ye may be able to bear it."
(1 Corinthians 10:13)

When you use drugs, you become subject to what the drugs want to do. They each have their own set of agendas and they do what they desire to do...through **YOU**.

Mary Jane (marijuana) wants to eat up all the food in the refrigerator when it's in control, and have a deep philosophical discourse with anyone who will give an ear.

Heroin wants to chill, nod, be real cool, and sleep for a second. Then it'll wake up, talk, and not care about anything nor anyone.

Cocaine wants to speed around the place and move quickly. It's suspicious of everyone and everything, and often chooses to stay away from others while in its 'hyper' state. It never wants to eat and will make you lose all of your curves and features that were explicitly yours. It's real touchy and loves being alone in a quiet space because it heightens your senses. While under the influence, you can hear things no one else hears. You just **KNOW** the police are coming to get you. You're suspicious of *everything* and *everybody*.

Crazy! Crazy! Crazy!

CONTAMINANT: LSD

This drug is "silly-bo-billy" and a potent hallucinogenic. It takes you on a journey as you sit in your living room or bedroom. It will not allow you to stop the journey nor go to sleep to escape the journey - but you wouldn't want to: it's weird and very colorful. I experienced no true addiction there because I didn't like "that" high. Thank God for **DELIVERANCE**!

#####

> *"Howbeit Jesus suffered him not, but saith unto him, 'Go home to thy friends, and tell them how great things the Lord hath done for thee, and hath had compassion on thee.' And he departed, and began to publish in Decapolis how great things Jesus had done for him: and all men did marvel."*
> (Mark 5:19-20)

I encourage you today: Share what has transpired in your life. Open your mouth and tell others! Testifying is vital to the Madman's (and Madwoman's) **DELIVERANCE**!

CHAPTER FIVE
Jesus' Marketing Plan

When the Madman was delivered in Mark 5, he wanted to go with Jesus, but Jesus told him 'No'. Jesus disclosed the greatest marketing plan for the Gospel **EVER** - and that included the Madman going and publishing (telling others) regarding his encounter with the Savior.

Sharing my life's story with you while unveiling my hidden past is like lying bare for everyone to stare upon while judging me and seeing my past faults. *HOWEVER*, if being naked before you helps you realize I'm living proof there is deliverance for **YOU**, your children, your business, or whatever area in which you need deliverance, then I've accomplished my goal!

We continue to overcome by the Blood of the Lamb and the word of our testimony (Revelation 12:11). If each one of us operates like the Madman, sharing the goodness of God in our lives, just think how encouraged and determined others will become - especially the generation that's coming along behind us!

> *I'M LIVING PROOF:*
> *THERE IS*
> *DELIVERANCE!*

Jesus' Marketing Plan

My mother prayed for me. She was so loving through the process of my being overcome by the spirit of addiction. In her love for me, she longed to see me free from the yoke of addiction. She sought help from every possible avenue.

Let her be an example. We should never **EVER** stop believing and doing what God directs us to do for the salvation and deliverance of our loved ones.

My older daughter prayed for me. My son was too young at the time to understand my addiction. God bless them both! *(My youngest daughter was not even a thought during my battle with drugs, thus no recollection of the 'old me'.)* Many times, I made my eldest tag along as I drove to the places where I'd purchase my drugs. When the car headed in that direction, she knew where we were going - and she hated it. She'd tell my mother and they would pray. Don't ever let anyone tell you prayer doesn't work! I did not receive manifestation of deliverance during the same timeframe in which they were praying; however, I am now delivered, and I believe it was due to their fervent prayers. My husband told my mother there was no hope for me, but apparently, he didn't know the power of a praying mother! He didn't know I'm encompassed about with those who are cheering me on…a great cloud of witnesses in the spirit realm (see Hebrews 12:1)! More importantly, he didn't know the power of a praying **Savior**.

"And who would dare tangle with God by messing with one of God's chosen? Who would dare to even point a finger? The One who died for us…the One who was raised to life for us…is in the presence of God at this very moment sticking up for us. Do you think anyone is going to be able to drive a wedge between us and Christ's love for us?"
(Romans 8:34)

CHAPTER SIX
Distractions, Distractions, and MORE Distractions!

How did a Beauty Queen First Runner-Up, a Sleeping Beauty actress in the school's performances, the articulate Sunday School Speech Presenter, Spelling Bee winner, Book Club participant, swimmer, Drill Team member, band member, piano, clarinet, and upright bass player fall for the "okidoke"? How did she get duked? Tricked? Hooked?

Now listen: Just as the Madman encountered whatever caused him to arrive at a place of cutting himself in the tombs, we too will encounter challenges in life. Some folks choose to end it all and commit suicide. **NOT US!**

Once we're set free from destructive behaviors, the battle for freedom will continue to ensue. You will need to learn to comply with the Rules of Engagement. ***STAY WITH THE WORD!*** It may *appear* that no help is coming. As you waste time on Facebook and other social media sites looking at what others are claiming fame to, you begin to think: *Is my day ever coming?* You have quickly forgotten from where and from what God has delivered you, and He'll do more…if you believe. The longer you lose focus, the longer your next phase of deliverance will take. However, a forward-thinking focus on where God is taking you to will create a faster arrival at your desired destiny.

Distractions, Distractions, and MORE Distractions!

How long have you been wanting some relief from whatever oppresses you? How many times have you sought Christ to help you, while it appears others are getting their breakthroughs and yours is being further delayed? It may **LOOK** like help is never coming, but I'm writing to let you know that at any time you decide you want **DELIVERANCE**, it happens **RIGHT THEN!**

The man, Jairus, sought help for his sick 12-year-old daughter. When it looked like all hope was lost, Jesus jacked Jairus' faith up and said, "**BE NOT AFRAID; ONLY BELIEVE!**" See, when you're waiting on what you're standing for, you've already sought help from God and fear is knocking at the door. It may **LOOK** like all hope is lost, but **BE NOT AFRAID! CONTINUE BELIEVING!**

When Jairus first asked Jesus for help, his daughter was still alive. All he wanted Jesus to do was lay hands on her, but Jesus' attention was on the woman with the 12-year issue of blood who had reached out in faith and received her deliverance. Jairus could have gotten mad at and upset with Jesus for allowing the woman to stop Him from getting to Jairus' house quicker, but he remained calm - even when the report came that his daughter had passed away. Jesus helped Jairus maintain what I call his 'Faith Focus' by telling him not to be afraid and to **ONLY BELIEVE!**

In Mark Chapter 5, we see Jesus has provided deliverance for the woman with the issue of blood *(she could have been killed for coming out into the streets in her condition)* **AND** Jesus also raised Jairus' daughter back to life.

When you truly believe Jesus has taken care of your situation, paid a price, and already provided a way of escape, you can stay in 'Faith Focus'. The question today is this: **Will you believe against all odds?**

Who'd A Thought Deliverance Would Come?

I once heard Joel Osteen say he was believing for the Compaq Center. The votes to allow it to become a church were slim to none; however, after a few years of losing sleep, battling the naysayers, and staying in faith, he and his congregation now have a model facility in a prime location - because he chose to **BELIEVE**. His mother, Dodie Osteen, believed she could defeat a terminal inoperable disease in her body approximately 30-40 years ago, and she's alive and very active today - traveling, having fun, ministering to others, and enjoying her life.

There you are. You have Jesus' attention. You can see manifestation is near. He's walking with you, but then someone with faith pulls Him in their direction and you're wanting to exclaim, *"COME ON, JESUS! I need you to take care of my situation right now!"* Along comes someone telling you it's too late; trouble not the Master anymore. You want to take your fists and beat up Jesus because you feel like He got sidetracked from keeping His promise to you. That is **NEVER** the case with Jesus. If He gets to your situation a year later, remember this: He created time, and everything will line up accordingly when Jesus is on the scene!

Why am I telling you about these distractions? **BECAUSE I WAS DEAD!** My first husband told my mom there was no hope for me. He told me I was obsessed with drugs *(and so was he, by the way)*, but he was never capable of seeing the beam in his own eye - only the mote or speck in mine (see Luke 6:41). However, I must admit: I was capable of generating more income than he. Therefore, my drug habit was much costlier than his. That is not important, though. What **IS** important is that I am **ALIVE** and have not used drugs for over 30 years! There's hope and deliverance for thousands of people enduring the epidemic of drug addiction today.

Distractions, Distractions, and MORE Distractions!

When you see an addict on the streets, in the workplace, or even in your home, please think of me and remember: Lucy was once just as they are, and the power of **GOD** transformed her life! No, I don't look like them. Everyone who is addicted to something is not always overt in their behavior and appearance regarding what they are entrapped with. Those who do show signs of what they are yoked up to, please treat them humanely because they are unable to set themselves free. It will take you speaking words of **DELIVERANCE** over their lives in order for them to be released. They are in the darkness and can't find the light on their own.

> *ALL OBESE PEOPLE ARE NOT FAT; NEITHER ARE ALL ADDICTS DOWNTRODDEN IN APPEARANCE.*

Sidebar: John Ramirez was once a man who worshipped Satan and became extremely powerful in the world of darkness. Today, he is a Minister of the Gospel of Jesus Christ. I heard him speak about his practices as a Satan-controlled man. He spoke about being up all night while being used by the devil as an instrument to influence evil by speaking addictions, evil, poverty, sex trade, and more over certain regions. He said, "*If Christians knew how powerful their words were, they would use them according to the Bible.*" He also shared the importance of praying in tongues and how the devil really hates that because he does not know what you're praying to God about. Those with that gift, he fights intensely.

Who'd A Thought Deliverance Would Come?

People may say there's no hope in any given situation. People may say he or she is dead and it's **OVER** for them. Our Lord and Savior, Jesus Christ, *STILL* has resurrection power and can raise any dead situation. **HE** can bring life back to that person again. **BELIEVE IT!**

Prophesy to those dead and unwanted situations in your life or your family member's life. Watch that situation be just as **YOU** call it (see Ezekiel 37:4-6).

CALL IT LIKE YOU WANT IT TO BE...NOT LIKE IT IS!

Remove the distractions!

CHAPTER SEVEN
They Laughed, BUT I Laughed Best!

Against all odds, **BELIEVE!** The Lord will put breath in you, and you will come to new life. No more dead and dry situations in need of deliverance…

I was tired of living that lifestyle. I was a good church girl, raised on good, old-fashioned fire-and-brimstone preaching. I had a personal encounter with Jesus Christ, the Lover of my early years. I told God I was tired and was not raised to live the life of a junkie. He heard me, too! He moved on my behalf! Just a small, private conversation with Him is all it took.

I remember going upstairs in the projects to get high at my friend's mother's home. As I climbed the stairs, I said, "Lord, I'm tired of being in this bondage. When are you going to send the police for me or someone to help me?" At the time, I thought deliverance only came through incarceration. I would see former junkies immediately after their release from jail or prison, and they looked healthy and free. However, many upon their release, engaged in and faced the same spiritual battles with addictions they had prior to being incarcerated. Still, that's how bad I wanted to be delivered. I was willing to go to jail!

People look at this physical house (my body) that I live in and they think they know me - but they don't **KNOW** me. I live inside my physical body (my house), and I thank God for the changes He has brought about in my life. There have been times when the 'Old Lucy' wanted to resurrect herself, and she was not always nice at all!

Who'd A Thought Deliverance Would Come?

Formerly, I was a very bright Christian girl who later indulged in promiscuity and a life of drugs and crime. Since then, I have been **DELIVERED**. People have taken advantage of me, stolen from me, lied on me, and done all manner of evil against me. I knew it, and God would have me retaliate by confessing the Word over what I was considering doing in response via my human nature. I cast down those wicked imaginations in Jesus' name and forgave them (as I thought of things to do to get my revenge). God said vengeance is **HIS**! He will repay! Therefore, I've learned to let Him fight my battles for me. That is no easy task. Sometimes, it seemingly takes Him a little longer than I'd like, but He's sovereign. We have to allow Him to be who He is because He knows the end before we know what's next! Remember: Just like He has a plan for your deliverance, He has a plan for the person who did you wrong…their deliverance as well.

Because I believed, they laughed! Let them laugh! We get the last laugh!

If there is one thing Pastor Creflo Dollar has taught me (among a laundry list of things) is to be delivered from 'People Bondage'.

Lucy 101

People are going to talk about you if you're playing your "A-game" or if you're not bringing the heat at all. They're going to throw you under the bus any and every opportunity they have - especially if they are not secure in their own skin. So, throw your head up as high as you can get it and constantly exercise Word-filled self-talk!

They Laughed, BUT I Laughed Best!

When you walk into a setting, carry yourself as if you own the joint - be it in the church, the office, or Starbucks. You are somebody because God doesn't make junk. Whatever it takes to keep your mind elevated to who you really are in Christ, do it! Refuse to downplay the masterpiece you really are - regardless of the silent verbal bricks that are hitting you all up side your head from gossipers. You can hear what people are not saying out loud if you're tuned in to God. Go on and strut your stuff, Woman of God! To the Men of God, lean on in and **SWAG!**

If you try to satisfy a bunch of naysayers, whisperers, and backbiters by not sharing your testimony…if you refuse to move forward with all God has predestined you to be in order to set someone else free, guess what?… You will offend the other bunch. If you try to do what the other bunch wants you to do, you'll offend the one who really knows what happened. If you try to please the one who wants you to tell it their way, you'll offend someone else. Be set **FREE**! Do what *GOD* instructs you to do and keep it moving.

At the end of the day, all that matters is the moment you stand before God and He asks, *"Did you do what I sent you to Earth to do?"* You will be able to say, **"YES!"**, so be free from people. Not being free from people is a form of *FEAR*. Fear is Satan's first name!

Let *them* laugh at you. Let *them* talk about you. **SO WHAT! GET OVER IT!** The world is so much larger than *them*.

Dr. Leroy Thompson likes to say, *"Roll your window up, keep going to the bank, and keep making deposits."* Haters were here when Jesus walked the Earth some 2,000 years ago. Don't think they just dropped off the planet…

Who'd A Thought Deliverance Would Come?

My favorite Spiritual Mom, Minister Betty Darnell, did an expository teaching on 'emulations'. What an enlightening message that was! Emulations are a higher form of jealousy! For example, if you have a Tesla, I must surpass you and take it to another level. I have to get a Bentley! Never being satisfied with or happy about what you have, you feel the need to continuously outdo your neighbor until it drains you, has you spending what you don't have, or ultimately kills you. When it's all said and done, what difference does it make anyway? Who cares about what you have? Get a life…a life in Christ! Stop trying to impress people who don't even care. **FAITH FOCUS!**

GET FREE! DELIVERANCE COMES!

CHAPTER EIGHT
Just Be FREE!

"And straightway the damsel arose, and walked; for she was of the age of twelve years. And they were astonished with a great astonishment."
(Mark 5:24)

That is just an example of the miracle-working power of God - something He did on **several** occasions throughout the Bible. He caused life to come back into the girl! **NO ONE** can deliver like our God! He's ready to do the same for you!

When you believe *and* expect it, **DELIVERANCE** comes!

Who'd A Thought Deliverance Would Come?

Imagine this: One day, you wake up and have no desire to do bad things anymore. One day, you wake up and trust God to take care of your children and bring them back into the fold. One day, you wake up and don't care what people think about you. One day, you wake up and you're more in love with Jesus than you've **EVER** been. Why? Because you've come to depend on the finished works of God. What He said in His Word is truth, and it is already done. It has the power to bring itself to pass, and it has already been fulfilled. You're not *GOING* to be healed; you are **ALREADY** healed - regardless of what the symptoms suggest! You're not *GOING* to be delivered from drugs; He who the Son sets free is free indeed! You're **ALREADY** delivered from drugs!

TAKE YOUR RIGHTFUL PLACE!
STEP INTO YOUR FREEDOM!

Just Be FREE!

The same holds true for a workaholic, adulterer, fornicator, or one who is hooked on pornography. You're **ALREADY** free! Just ask God to help your unbelief and receive the finished works of Jesus Christ! When He died on the cross, He said, *"It is finished!"* Now you know what He meant! He knew you were going to be outrageous, so He went ahead and paid the price in full for you to walk in wholeness and fullness - nothing missing, nothing broken, and nothing lacking in your life! He's not going back to get on that cross **ever** again. He paid for what you did wrong yesterday. He paid for what you did wrong today. And guess what? He paid for what you will do wrong tomorrow because He loves you!

"For mothers and fathers believing God for their children, know this, they are delivered through the cleanness of your hands."
(Job 22:30)

"Also, the seed of the righteous shall be delivered!"
(Proverbs 11:21)

As a Woman of God, only a woman can show me where a fine man of God is. That's the bottom line. The devil tries to keep us in darkness with our sinful past, causing us to feel shame. We need to be free and tell others about the saving grace of God. You're not the only one he (the devil) influenced to do dirty deeds, but he wants you to **THINK** you are.

I'm here to love and shed light. I don't know everyone's story, but I do know God loves them, just like He loved me out of sin. You must remember this: *IT'S ALL SIN!*

My dad spoke words over me at birth, regretting I was not a boy. Some would say what he said was labeling or even satanically influenced. Later, during my addiction, I allowed evil spirits to use me in ways that were unbecoming of the good, Christian girl I am - the now-**DELIVERED** girl!

Who'd A Thought Deliverance Would Come?

"Sin will take you farther than you want to go, make you stay longer than you want to stay, and cost you more than you want to pay!"

Words play into our actions in a *powerful* way. My Spanish teacher told me during my second year of taking his class in 7th grade (when I was unable to effectively translate what he spoke to me in Spanish) that I looked like something that fell off the back end of a truck. **WORDS** can be like daggers - or if used properly they can build one up. For a 7th-grader, his chastisement was detrimental; however, I wish he could look at me now!

I sang the following song as a little Church girl regularly on Sunday mornings:

"Come into my heart, Lord Jesus! Come in today. Come in to stay. Come into my heart, Lord Jesus!"

Thank God He stayed with me through all the drugs, all the sin, all the lies, and all the dishonesty that so easily beset me…

THANK YOU, LORD!

Use Your Time Wisely to Maintain Your New Life… Your Deliverance Requires Maintenance

An Olympiad college student who studied between each practice session for the Olympics then went on to win the Gold while maintaining a 4.0 GPA is an example of one using time wisely. Making the most of every moment, she would go underneath the bleachers to read and study until she was called for her next round of exercises on the beam.

Don't tell me there's not enough time in the day to meditate and imagine for 15 to 20 minutes!

Just Be FREE!

Don't tell me there's not enough time to read books that promote healthy roots and thoughts for 15 to 30 minutes a day!

Don't tell me there's not enough time to work out with an online yoga class or a walking DVD for 15 to 30 minutes a day!

Don't tell me there's not enough time to change the course of your life by making investments in yourself and ridding yourself of emotional rollercoaster craziness!

It's time to nourish your spirit, soul, and body with new things and new activities. **KILL PROCRASTINATION!** Procrastination is a thief of time. Be a *PHOENIX*! Rise up from the ashes!

Who'd A Thought Deliverance Would Come?

Thank God for DELIVERANCE!

DELIVERANCE from good works...trying to be Miss Goodie Two-Shoes.

DELIVERANCE from sin...trying to self-destruct.

DELIVERANCE from bondage...being yoked up to sin and drugs.

DELIVERANCE from people and their poor measure of themselves...attempting to project their image on you.

DELIVERANCE from small thinking...thinking only of something you can accomplish on your own.

DELIVERANCE from food addictions, anorexia, gluttony, etc.

DELIVERANCE from drugs...abusive substances and their accompanying rituals.

DELIVERANCE from shopaholism...out-of-control addiction to shopping.

DELIVERANCE from workaholism...hiding from family and other responsibilities by always working.

DELIVERANCE from alcoholism...overindulgence in alcohol.

GET. SET. FREE!

Forgive yourself!

Repeat this over and over again until you "get it":

"I am forgiven and I forgive MYSELF!"

CHAPTER NINE
Beautified and Dignified

There was a time when I considered aborting this book, but I am here now giving birth to my 'Book Baby'. God delivered me so I could tell you my truth: My life was truly jacked up until **He** sorted it all out.

HE BEAUTIFIED AND DIGNIFIED ME!

He makes all things beautiful in His time. He made me, and I am **SO** beautiful (see Ecclesiastes 3:11). He wants you to be ready when He comes for you - and you must be ready! Let Him clean you up and make all things new in your life.

If you faint in the day of adversity, your strength is small. God needs you to know who you are. Eagles, for example, are very powerful. At a certain point in time after their birth, they are *forced* to learn how to fly. If the eaglet has challenges, the parent eagle is there to fly underneath and help it to not crash. The attempts at flying are ongoing until the eaglet gets it right. Doesn't that sound like our Heavenly Father? He wants us to **soar**! It's a whole lot easier to do so when you're **FREE** - delivered and rid of all unnecessary baggage and challenges!

Thank God for erasers on pencils! You and I have made mistakes in life. We have the Blood of Jesus to cleanse us from **ALL** sin! Yes: I've had a horrible past. Today, I rarely give it any thought because that is not who I am any longer. I live on a steady diet of the Word of God because where I'm going and what I'm accomplishing requires an enormous amount of **FAITH FOCUS.** The way to where I want to arrive requires the techniques I'm sharing with you.

Who'd A Thought Deliverance Would Come?

"Faith comes by hearing, and hearing by the Word of God" (Romans 10:17). If it takes faith to get you to where you want to go, you will definitely need to be hearing, reading, believing, speaking, and living the Word of God. To get there, please realize the secret of your future is in your **daily** routines. To refresh your memory, they should include:

- Meditating/Imagining
- Reading
- Exercising
- FAITH FOCUS

The books you read and the people you associate with will play a major role in where you'll end up in the next few years. The exact quote from Charles "Tremendous" Jones reads, *"You are the same today that you are going to be five years from now except for two things: the people with whom you associate and the books you read."*

> *YOU ARE THE SAME TODAY THAT YOU ARE GOING TO BE FIVE YEARS FROM NOW EXCEPT FOR TWO THINGS: THE PEOPLE WITH WHOM YOU ASSOCIATE AND THE BOOKS YOU READ."*

Looking back on my life and thinking about some of the men I would teach in the prisons when I'd visit them as a part of the Prison Ministry from my church, I would tell them they needed to stop going through that revolving door. Children enjoy playing with revolving doors and merry-go-rounds, but adults have a destination to reach. If they have to go through the revolving door and allow it to serve its purpose, then so be it; but from there, go forward! Some people don't know how to get off the 'incarceration rollercoaster/merry-go-round' (better known in the legal world as 'recidivism')!

Albert Einstein defined insanity as 'doing the same thing over and over again and expecting different results'.

> **INSANITY: DOING THE SAME THING OVER AND OVER AGAIN AND EXPECTING DIFFERENT RESULTS.**

One bad decision after another. One failed relationship after another. One arrest after another. One lie after another. One bad high after another. One disappointment after another. One too many drinks after another. One more broken promise after another.

That was my life…

UNTIL I asked JESUS to help me - and He did just that!

Who'd A Thought Deliverance Would Come?

All of a sudden, I didn't frequent the places I was addicted to going to anymore. You see, drug and alcohol addictions are not stand-alone habits; they have associates. You don't only become addicted to the drug, but the whole ordeal:

- Knowing the drug man.
- Knowing the slang and secret places the dope man is going to be found.
- Copping the drug.
- Smelling the drugs as you use them.
- The feelings associated with the drugs.
- The desires that come as a result of the drugs.
- The conversations and attraction to life in the fast lane.

The hustle to get money to purchase drugs is also a part of the "get high every day" experience. You fall in love with the rituals and allow them to become the experiences you seek several times a day - depending on how entangled you are with the stronghold of the yoke the enemy has placed around your neck that is attached to his.

YOKED!

Spirits must have bodies in which to carry out their assignments. **YOU** are a spirit and you live inside your body; however, in order for evil spirits to successfully carry out their missions, they seek someone - *a body* - to perform their guile through...someone who is open and vulnerable.

The spirit of adultery needs a body. The spirit of thievery needs a body. The spirit of addiction needs a body. The spirit of gluttony needs a body. The spirit of alcoholism needs a body. The spirit of lying needs a body. The spirit of murder needs a body...and so on, and so on.

As for **ME**? I'm *FREE*! Therefore, I'm always smiling! I'm having constant communion (internal conversations) with the One who delivered me from all of that crap - the One who has taken me to a level in Him that affords me such a luxurious, loving state of **BEING**!

I want parents to know: God is a Deliverer, and He **WILL** deliver your children. He promised in His Word: "*...the seed of the righteous shall be delivered...*" (Proverbs 11:21).

My family thought there was no hope for me. My first husband thought there was no hope for me. I was the one who excelled in school, was very respectful, went to college, grew up in Sunday School, and attended church regularly. I am the one who became the first Doctor in my family.

Who'd A Thought Deliverance Would Come?

It doesn't matter how locked up you are - whether it is with food, drugs, or anything else. Remember: **GOD** has the power to set you free.

When my deliverance was manifested, I was at church 24/7. I found home Bible studies to attend. My spirit was so hungry for sound doctrine and teaching from the Word of God. I had starved myself for so long from that which gave me **LIFE**!

Who'd A Thought Deliverance Would Come?

Although I sold out to God, there were some who were not genuinely sold out to the things of God. They were church-goers who (when they saw the lasting change in my life) began to 'hate on me'. I was even called "Holier than Thou".

I had to terminate old drug relationships because I had no desire to do what they did any longer. My oldest daughter began to rebel, after having prayed for me all of those years. She had come into her teens at the same time God was delivering me - and the enemy was **HOT** on her trail! I refused to let him have her. I began to pray for her, just as she had prayed for me. It hasn't been easy standing in **FAITH FOCUS** mode for my children; however, **STILL I STAND!** I'm out there serving God and working with Young Life after I became free, working to save other teens. The enemy was working **OVERTIME** in his attempts to steal mine!

Allow me a moment to share something with you…

Once you're delivered - set free from whatever you're standing against - the enemy of your soul will come with other attempts to **DESTROY** you. You will have to stand against and annihilate him for attacking you. I've learned that life is an ongoing series of events with victories that require battles!

You win over cigarettes; you battle overeating!

You win over drugs; you battle shame!

You win over gossip; you battle not being included in conversations!

You win with weight loss; you struggle with not reaching the perfect size!

Beautified and Dignified

You win with a spouse returning to a severed marriage; you struggle with who the spouse was with during the separation; additionally, the comparison trap... Were they better than me?

You win over pornography; you battle with the mind games from the residue!

You win with that new promotion; you battle with the stress associated with increased responsibilities!

You win with riches and wealth; you battle with who's stealing from you!

Life is a *BATTLE*...**BUT** the good news is this: **WE WIN!**

As I came out of my old life and into my new, there were distractions. I sought a support system in my local church. The Pastor of my neighborhood church made advances towards me in a manner that was not conducive with the lifestyle change I had begun. The devil did not want to let go of me! *BUT...*

"And it shall come to pass in that day, that his burden shall be taken away from off thy shoulder, and his yoke from off thy neck, and the yoke shall be destroyed because of the anointing."
(Isaiah 10:27)

The invisible yoke the enemy had around my neck previously was destroyed by the power of **GOD**! I did not allow myself to be lured back into an ungodly yoke - inside **OR** outside of the church!

Sometimes, you have to **FIGHT** for your deliverance. Parents, no matter how bad it looks, you have a promise from **GOD** that the seed of the righteous shall be delivered! It's a **DONE DEAL!**

Who'd A Thought Deliverance Would Come?

For parents believing God for their children, know this: According to Job 22:30, they will be delivered through the cleanness of your hands. Continue to believe God for their deliverance. Keep your hands clean...and watch God bring them right on home! "Home" means not only your physical house, but back to the things of God - back to the mind of Christ. That is **FAITH FOCUS**, especially if they are anything like I *WAS*. ☺

Children, do not give up on your parents. Your parents go through a lot, and they are growing just as you are growing. Parents don't know it all. God saved me and made me a much better parent. If only you will *BELIEVE*, He will do the same for **your** parents. However, if you are in danger, then you need to believe for some good temporary parental figures until the deliverance work is completed in your "present" parents.

Jesus paid a price so that we will not have to be abused. For those of you who are not born again and have not received Christ in your life, you can be healed, too! You can be delivered, too! You see, God is **LOVE** (see John 3:16). He loves you so much, He sent His ***ONLY*** Son for you - even while you were in 'Sin City', so don't feel like He won't deliver you if you ask for deliverance. He cares for you just that much!

Understand this: I was not acting like a Christian when I was strung out on heroin and cocaine, but when I genuinely cried out for help, God was right there!

Beautified and Dignified

I beg of you: Get delivered and experience life like you never thought it could be. Then, get saved by asking Jesus to come into your life. I promise it will be a ride like no other. You will then need to receive another gift He has for you called the Baptism of the Holy Spirit with the evidence of speaking in tongues. *(I used to think people who did that were off their rockers; however, it gives you the supernatural ability to pray about things you were unable to pray about in your own understanding.)*

For example, your spouse may be tempted to cheat on you. As you're praying in the Holy Spirit (some call Him the Holy Ghost), you can stop the activity of your spouse that could ultimately create disharmony in your marriage. Praying in the Spirit will allow you to get answers - ones you had no idea about previously. The Spirit is your secret partner…a true force to be reckoned with…a **REAL** "Know It All"…and a Best Friend. He's your answer to unanswerable situations. He's hilarious, but oh so powerful. He's your invisible guide and **ALWAYS** with you.

Once you're delivered, you've gotten saved, and have been baptized in the Holy Spirit, **GO SHARE THE GOOD NEWS WITH SOMEONE ELSE!** Don't keep all of that goodness to yourself!

How did I - a child with so much promise - turn out to be so horrible? One bad seed or negative influence sown into my life and allowed to take root (without having the Word of God's seed to uproot and overtake it) produced a mighty harvest of bad. Not only that, but we are born in this world as sinners, shapen in iniquity by our surroundings and environment. However, after we accept Christ, we are born again and begin to renew our minds to the abundant way of living we were created to enjoy.

Who'd A Thought Deliverance Would Come?

When you abuse drugs or alcohol, your mind is easily-altered from making sound decisions. Even in my addicted state, I had values. There were certain things I was not going to do. I held fast to my values for a very long time - until a prominent drug dealer once required otherwise. I let myself down and vowed to never engage in that "required activity" ever again.

Note: When you let yourself down - even while on drugs - you feel extremely bad.

When I was young, I saw a Playboy magazine that had a picture of the first African American Miss America exposed in the centerfold with another woman. I looked up to her in my youth! She was, after all, on cereal boxes! *What in the world was I doing looking at Playboy?* Well, they were once on the shelves in the drug stores, and my male buddy would steal them! We would then go over the near the church and look through the magazines. Oh my goodness! I guess we thought we'd be safe looking at nude pictures near the church. **WOW!**

Even as a drug addict, I knew Jesus prior to the addiction. I knew certain things were not pleasing to God, and I prayed for Him to deliver me from them all. I am an Exhorter - one who encourages others. I am always building people up. It is common for me to compliment both men and women, as it is in my nature to do so. It's funny how people in the church will embrace and embellish things they've heard (mind you, hearsay only), but you must remember this: The devil goes to church regularly, too! He doesn't want you to go to church, so he will do whatever he can to deter you. Give him **NO** place! We are to forsake not the assembling of ourselves together. In other words, the Bible says we are to go to church!

Beautified and Dignified

When Jesus moved into my life and I sold out to Him, I stayed in my Bible and in strong Word of Faith teachings from People of God such as: Kenneth Hagin, Norvel Hayes, Oral Roberts, John Osteen, Kenneth Copeland, Willie Bolden, Fred Price, Joyce Meyer, Creflo Dollar, T.D. Jakes, Bill Winston, Jerry Savelle, and Jesse Duplantis. I have sat under their teachings for a very long time and, of course, along the way, I received revelation from others - but my main focus of learning came from the above referenced Ministers of the Gospel. I've been seeking God a long time and have **YET** to exhaust all that He continues to reveal Himself to me as.

I didn't quit the Word, and the Word didn't quit me. The Word of God taught me how to dress modestly and how to apply my makeup like a child of God should - *NOT* like I'm ready to go out to the nightclub during the day or stand on the street corner! LOL! The Holy Spirit will teach you a great deal if you will take the time to listen to and acknowledge Him. He's taught me how to eat, make healthy choices, and so much more.

Back to the main point: Once I began to be taught from the People of God, all of the old spirits, old habits, and old ways of thinking were evicted. I was set **FREE** from that old, sinful nature.

You see, the devil will try to keep you in darkness with constant recollection of your sinful past, trying to make you feel shame. Jesus took your shame (see Isaiah 61:7)! When someone takes your shame, it's been **TOOK** - not taken! ☺ Jesus paid an awesome price for me to be free and not feel guilt; thus, I am truly *FREE*! No more shame is holding me.

Who'd A Thought Deliverance Would Come?

Realize this: You will never please everyone, but you can help *someone* when you tell them how the Lord has delivered you. Don't hide in the darkness. Come on out into the light! God's saving grace is amazing! *'Who'd A Thought'* you've been through what you've been through?

Know **THIS**: We're not the only ones the devil has influenced to do things he would like for us to keep hidden in the dark so he can 'lord' over us. The devil wants you to think you are the only one whom he was successful in influencing to do dirty deeds, but he is a **LIAR**! He influenced others, but they are afraid of what others will think of them if they encourage someone else with their testimony of how God has delivered them.

I was so proud of one young lady who stood up in church the first Sunday I came to Atlanta. My children and I were visiting. Testimony time came, and this strikingly gorgeous young lady stood with her strong, powerful-looking husband alongside her holding their child. When she began to speak, she thanked God for delivering her from a strong sex drive that caused her to have sex with everyone on an **entire** NFL (professional football) team. Mouths dropped, but she was **FREE**! She had received her deliverance, and she shared her testimony in what she deemed to be a safe environment. She wanted others to know how much God loves us.

God, help the church!

Recently in the news, coaches hiring ladies to have sex with draft picks they desired for their football and basketball teams were exposed. Looks like we have some *MORE* things to pray about…

Beautified and Dignified

Another thing I'd like to share with you: Those who will remain in darkness will point the finger at you - the one who is now free and living in the light. They will say, *"She/He is the one who did drugs! She/He is the one who participated in illicit sex!"* Know that they are human and only talking about and pointing the finger at you because the evil one still has influence in their lives. Just practice responding with, **"I'm the one Jesus set FREE!"**

I knew another young lady who shared her testimony with me regarding the use of abortion as a form of birth control. She's free now and is a very beautiful, professional, and productive Woman of God. Deliverance came to her! She no longer participates in sex outside of marriage, and she knows she will see all of those babies once she gets to Heaven.

People find it so much easier to magnify negative acts rather than positive ones. Although I've been set free from all of those past sins for over 30 years, there are relatives I still see today who say to me, *"Remember when you used to be strung out?"* One time, I attended a family function. I drove over an hour to get there and was accompanied by my children. When I arrived, there were relatives who greeted me - and it felt so good. I complimented one of the relatives I hadn't seen in a long time (remember, I'm an Exhorter by nature). I simply said, *"You look so pretty!"* (She had her hair done up so nicely and she looked healthy.) Another relative began to act in a manner that was totally over-the-top and said, *"Oh, no: You can't have her!"* - indicating I was attracted to my female relative. I was so taken back, I wanted to retreat, take my children, and leave - but we must learn to endure hardness as a good soldier. Never cower and run away from the enemy of your soul. That was the reason he had her say that. His goal was to try to get me to react. Learn to **IGNORE** the devil.

I completely ignored the comment and continued visiting with the rest of my relatives. I had a good time, ate some good country cooking, and, when the function was over, drove back home and had a good night's rest.

Forgive and Forget!

You must know the devil is going to try to remind you at every turn about what you did bad because he influenced you to do it, but you must also know who you are in Christ. You are accepted in the beloved! You are the apple of God's eye! His thoughts of you are many. He has you before His eyelids. He loves you, and you must love yourself. Learn to let people have their opinions, but make sure you know the truth about you! Be comfortable in your own skin. **LOVE YOURSELF!** You're of a royal priesthood with royal blood flowing through your veins. You are the righteousness of God in Christ Jesus. You are a new creation. You are the head and not the tail. You are seated in Heavenly places in Christ Jesus. You are more than a conqueror. You are beautiful. You are blessed and highly-favored with God and man. You are made in His image and His likeness. You are all that and then some!

AMEN!

CHAPTER TEN
It's Time to Renew Your Mind

The Bible says to forsake not the assembling of yourselves together (in other words, **GO TO CHURCH!**), so much more as you see the day approaching…and we do see the day approaching! Jesus is surely coming back; however, you need to go to church in order to renew your mind.

When you received Jesus, your spirit was made brand new, but your mind was in need of being renewed. By going to church, you learn how you are supposed to live your new life. Now, don't go to just **ANY** church! Go where *GOD* directs you to attend. Oh! Don't think the enemy is going to let you go. Don't think he's not going to try to hinder you. He will cause a fight between you and your spouse, or he will cause the children to get dirty right before you walk out the door. He may even cause the usher to treat you unkindly. The Pastor may say something that cuts you to the core and you will think, "*Who told him my business?*" Nevertheless, just keep going to church! When you go, give some money, too! They do, after all, have bills to pay! ☺

God tells us if we received spiritual things, then we are to give of our carnal things. For example, the Pastor who brings forth the Word is worthy of being compensated. In addition to that, the light bill, water bill, bathroom tissue, building maintenance, hymn books, TV screens, microphones, and choir robes - in addition to many other expenses - costs money!

Who'd A Thought Deliverance Would Come?

MORE importantly, when you give money to the church, you are making an investment into more sanctuaries for God to live in. Hear this: *God doesn't live in the church.* He lives in people who receive Him. The way people are compelled to allow Christ to come and live inside of them is when they hear a good teaching on the radio, television, in church on Sunday morning, at a camp meeting, or at an outreach function. Guess what? It takes money for all of those avenues to be set up so that you, I, and others who need a Savior will be able to hear and receive. So, give your money so God can have more sanctuaries (or temples/bodies) to dwell in! Okay?

When you get to Heaven, someone may come up to you and say, "*You gave $20.00 in church one Sunday and it paid for a biblical tract I received while in jail. That tract saved my life! Hallelujah!*"

We used to sing the following little song during Summer Bible School:

> "Come into my heart.
> Come into my heart.
> Come into my heart, Lord Jesus.
> Come in today.
> Come in to stay.
> Come into my heart, Lord Jesus."

The only way He gets to come in is if you hear someone talking about Him, then faith comes and you decide to invite Him in. So, let's give our money to keep the Word going out on every available wave! People will continue to have their lives changed for all eternity because we give! This thing called 'life' is wrapping up. The end is nearer than it was previously, and we need to attract as many souls as we can into the Kingdom of Almighty God! My desire is that none should be lost - and it's also God's desire.

It's Time to Renew Your Mind

You know, I had Jesus in my heart before I engaged in a life of crime and drugs. How did that happen? You and I have an enemy. It's not important how he influenced us. What's important is how we get set free from him: by the **POWER** of **JESUS CHRIST!** Thank God! He stayed with me through all the drugs, all the sin, all the lies, and all the dishonesty!

Remember in Mark 5, as Jairus came to Christ for help? It's not important that the man's daughter was at the point of death or how she got sick. Jesus healed her and brought her back to life! **THAT'S** important! Let's not focus on what caused the illness, drug addiction, or other sinful nature. Let's *FAITH FOCUS* on getting people the help they need!

DELIVERANCE CAME! GLORY TO GOD!

Don't be so overtaken with how the sin came into someone's life. Glorify God and allow Him to be manifested (see John 9:1-3).

The Madman of Gadarenes was found in the graveyard cutting himself. It is not important how he got in that situation. What's important is that Jesus set him free and gave him new life! The Madman wasn't mad anymore! He became a walking, talking marketing tool for the Gospel of Jesus Christ!

DELIVERANCE CAME! GLORY TO GOD!

Thank God for deliverance from trying to earn my salvation through good works!

Who'd A Thought Deliverance Would Come?

DELIVERANCE from Sin!

DELIVERANCE from Bondage!

DELIVERANCE from Small Thinking!

DELIVERANCE from Food Addictions!

DELIVERANCE from Backstabbing!

DELIVERANCE from Sitting Here Until I Die!

"Why sit ye here until you die, Lucy? Seek the Savior! He can help you, girl!" (See 2 Kings 7:3)

I am forgiven!

I forgive myself!

Woohoo!

CHAPTER ELEVEN
Pie in the Sky!

"If you faint in the day of adversity - and there will be days of adversity - your strength is small!"
Proverbs 24:10

Don't cave in! Don't give up! Don't quit!

I'm not going to sit here and tell you that living the Christian Faith Life according to the Gospel of Grace is going to be 'pie in the sky'. Then again, I might! When it's all said and done and we are out of here, it **WILL** be *'PIE IN THE SKY'!* ☺

What I want you to know is that when you live this Christian life, you will encounter challenges. Be happy, knowing Jesus has already defeated anything that comes against you. If you will just believe, you will see the goodness of the Lord while in the land of the living.

I'm certain that somewhere in your life, you have encountered a situation when you felt there was no way out. Now, you look back on it and guess what? It is all settled and over! That should be a lesson to you that you are to keep the faith in all circumstances. God will deliver you because He said the righteous are never forsaken nor their seed begging bread. He wants to treat you like you **NEVER** sinned. That's His *GRACE!*

Who'd A Thought Deliverance Would Come?

People will hate on you and do malicious acts against you. Why? Because they allow the devil to use their body to do his work! He does not have a body, so he goes around like a roaring lion - seeking whom he may destroy. Don't let him use you. When you see someone being used by him, take authority and bind up those spirits that would operate against you in the name of Jesus! You bind them up with the words you speak from your mouth in the authority of the Name that is above every name, and that is Jesus Christ! Yes! **YOU** have authority over those spirits!

(Note: It's not just crack addicts who have allowed him access. There are some corporate executives who have given him room and board, too!)

The following is worth repeating:

Sin will take you farther than you want to go, make you stay longer than you want to stay, and make you pay more than you want to pay!

Stop sinning! Love God enough to want to please Him in all that you do.

Let me share some of what I've encountered along life's path:

I've had a gun pulled on me and was threatened to be shot.

I've been beaten beyond recognition and hospitalized.

I've been convicted of crimes I didn't commit.

I've been divorced *AND* I've divorced. Each time, it hurt - no matter which one of us initiated it.

Pie in the Sky!

None of that moves me! Those little afflictions work a far better weight in Glory! Believe me when I say: You work through it. You're more powerful thank you think!

I've been treated indifferently by friends and family. I've experienced some really painful, disheartening things. The most painful I have ever encountered was in the house of the Lord...church! Church is a place where you go to receive consolation and lay your burdens down; however, to go there and be treated like an outsider and to have people blatantly lie on you is nothing but a trick of the enemy to get you to stop going to the place where your life support awaits. Don't ever stop going...**EVER!**

Here are some suggestions for superb books to help keep you **FAITH FOCUSED:**

Pilgrim's Progress by John Bunyan

Hind's Feet in High Places by Hannah Hurnard

The Hiding Place by Corrie Ten Boon

Still Doing the Impossible by Oral Roberts

The Alchemist by Paulo Coelho

These are some of the books I read initially upon my deliverance to help renew and readjust my thinking processes. It was a long time ago, but they are still masterpieces that work well today. Since that time, I've read hundreds of books - including reading my Bible daily. One that is an easy read and extremely encouraging is *Your Best Life Now* by Joel Osteen.

Who'd A Thought Deliverance Would Come?

DELIVERANCE IS HERE!

Remind yourself often of the following statement:

"I was created to make someone else's life better."

God wants us to love like He loves. He is always about delivering someone, healing someone, and drawing someone out of bad situations into good ones. In so doing, He's preparing temples for Himself to reside in...loving on someone, blessing someone, favoring someone, picking someone up, exalting someone, promoting someone, increasing someone, and giving life to someone...the door is usually opened for Him to come in and set up residency.

After having gone through all I've encountered in my life, I know God did not allow me to go through all of that for my own benefit. He helped me endure hardness as a good soldier in order to be able to tell you, so that you can draw strength from me. How? You see and now know that God delivered me, so surely, He can handle your situation, also! You can be victorious!

Pie in the Sky!

I have been treated unkindly by a Supervisor during employment at church. Not only in the arena of duties and responsibilities, but blatantly lied on and threatened by her. It was real messy. She was being used by the devil! I respected her just as David did Saul. I could have brought the situation to others, but I chose to take the high road and pray. I must be honest here and say in the moment, I really wanted to jump on her and beat her down! Had I reacted that way, both of us would likely have been fired. I had no fear, due to having dealt with similar demons in worldly settings. That supervisor did not move me. Do not fear! The mistreatment and the inexcusable lying were all part of a plan used to motivate me to leave **THAT** career and follow God's plan.

Let the Lord fight your battles.

I lived through the mistreatment and lies. You will **NEVER** guess what happened: The Lord allowed me to move into a new career! My salary tripled in the first year after leaving that woman and her madness. I really had matured! ☺ It's rewarding to see how far I've come in this walk with Christ.

During my Doctoral studies, I found there is a 'Fundamental State of Leadership' which one enters from time to time that affords one the opportunity to lead or thrive in a manner that is contrary to your normal character. You are in a zone that is not 'you', but you are totally aware. I believe that is God's grace affording you the opportunity to move beyond what is reality and rise above to do greater things.

I didn't get caught up in the trap that was being set for me on that job because He promised He would provide a way of escape. I used the attacks as stepping stones to move into the next arena God had for me.

Who'd A Thought Deliverance Would Come?

Use the resources you have to be empowered to do greater things. Don't get bogged down in the right and wrong of things. Instead, look inside to find out what's in store for you next!

I recall one year, I did not have the finances to keep my daughter in a wonderful private school. We believed God. We prayed. We sowed sacrificial offerings. Much to our surprise, she had to attend a neighborhood public elementary school. We were disappointed; however, we did not allow that to stop us from having our love for and continued relationship with God. Two years later, my daughter was soaring in a much better, prestigious private school where she thrived! God provided all of the necessary resources. While she was in the public school, she was used mightily by God to minister throughout the student body and on local cable channels through a competition she won. She spoke of her relationship with the Lord, giving people an opportunity to hear about Jesus and to choose life with Him.

God has a plan, my sister and brother. Sometimes it doesn't feel good following His plan, but He **IS** the Master Planner!

CHAPTER TWELVE
Believe Me: BELIEVE!

So, as you reflect back on my story, I'm sure you're asking, *"Why would I want to be a believer with all of the challenges **SHE'S** encountered in her walk with the Lord?"* WHY? Because you know there's eternity! You want to be on the winning side! You do not want to be left out! Going to Heaven and living your best life **EVER** in a mansion decorated with all the pleasures and décor you personally desire awaits you. Being in total bliss and a perfect atmosphere 24/7 with nothing but love emanating from everyone all of the time is a picture of living the perfect, heavenly life far beyond your wildest dreams.

"This light affliction worketh a far better weight in Glory!"
(2 Corinthians 4:17)

Jesse Duplantis' account of Heaven, the Throne Room of God, and the power of God is something I can't miss. I must see God, and I will not allow any of the petty challenges and circumstances that life delivers separate me from the love of God and all He has in store for me - not while I'm here on Earth, nor when I get to Heaven.

NOTE: I do not think we will encounter challenges in Heaven. ☺

Heaven is a real place. I've always wanted to be loved, and I've had a glimpse of what love is like; however, I will know love fully when I get to Heaven. Think of your happiest moments, surprises, best gifts, someone's random acts of kindness towards you, and all the joyous moments you've **EVER** experienced - all rolled into one...*FOREVER*! That's what Heaven will be like 24/7! **I LOVE THE VISION!**

Who'd A Thought Deliverance Would Come?

My parents are in Heaven. I know they are so happy they received Jesus into their lives while they were here on Earth. I did not take a chance on thinking my parents had received Jesus just because they took me to church as a little girl. I asked them (prior to their departing their earthly bodies) whether or not they had received Jesus Christ as their personal Lord and Savior. I simply asked, "*Have you ever asked Jesus to come into your heart?*" I was assured they had done so. If they had replied 'no', I was prepared to usher them into the sheepfold right then and there. Leave nothing to chance. **NEVER EVER ASSUME ANYTHING** - especially as it relates to salvation and eternity for yourself or someone else.

My mom had a bout with brain cancer. When she found out about it days after she retired, the Lord clearly shared with me that I needed to tell her to forgive my dad - to release him from all the unforgiveness for the things he had done against her. I don't know what those things were, but I presume it was related to infidelity…maybe. Again, I cannot say with 100% certainty. I went to her and told her what the Lord said: "*You need to release daddy and forgive him.*" She shook her head from side to side as if to say, "No!" Then, tears began streaming down her face. It is my belief the Lord wanted to heal her of the brain cancer, but she did not want to let go of past hurts before her transition to Heaven.

It is my belief that spirits of unforgiveness and other negative evil spirits are tied to sickness and disease. They work overtime to cause manifestation in one's physical area, normally in the area that houses the sin nature.

Believe Me: BELIEVE!

For my mom, it was in her thought-life; thus, the cancer formed in her brain. Some have challenges with not loving others. They house hatred in their hearts; thus, opening the door for heart problems. Others have had abortions; thus, cancers are associated with expelling a fetus or in their breasts. It must be noted here: The spirits that operate behind diseases can be expelled. Take authority over them as Jesus did in Mark 5 with the Madman! Cast them out, never to return again. Send them someplace else, but give them **NO** place in you.

As for me, when I locate an area in my life that may harbor a negative thought or spirit, I quickly repent and command that thing to leave my body - in **JESUS'** name! We've been given the authority - in the name of Jesus - to cast out demons. **USE IT!**

My Pastor's Mother-in-Law says, "*Don't let anyone rent space in your mind.*"

Kenneth Hagin says, "*A bird can fly over your head [thoughts], but don't let it build a nest in your hair [take up residency]!*"

People on drugs are sick - just like those addicted to working **ALL** of the time; or those who have cancer, or mental illness. When you're sick, you sometimes don't know it (you're in denial). You can't see you're in need of healing. In Luke 6:19, they were all seeking to touch Jesus and get healed. As I reached for Him, virtue and healing were released from Him to me. Yes, there are anointed doctors to help one get healed; however, they are practicing physicians. Jesus gives them insight. Hosea Chapter Five states, "*...some were healed and others were cured.*" **BOTH** take an act of faith. Guess what? ***GOD DOES BOTH OF THEM!***

Who'd A Thought Deliverance Would Come?

Many of you will judge me after reading some of the things I've shared about myself. I made a conscious decision to do so in order for you to know how far Jesus is willing to reach down and save. Still, my concern is not to focus on what you think about me; it is only to help those desiring to be set free.

Rahab the Harlot is in the lineage of Jesus Christ. Do you think Jesus allowed his prostitute relative to stop Him from reaching His full potential? Focus on getting set free from the bondage that holds you back from your full potential! We must change - every single one of us. Nothing stays the same. Without change, we never come to know our exceptional capabilities. Many times, change and growth are painful, but vitally necessary.

I have family - just like you. I have friends - just like you. Who wants to get naked in front of their family and friends while allowing the world to see what God has delivered you from? I believe God allowed me to go through all of that trash and filth because He knew I'd be obedient and tell it all. It is my prayer that your child, relative, or co-worker can be ministered to through this book and that you'd have an opportunity to see there is hope for your loved-one(s).

Believe Me: BELIEVE!

Grace has taught me so much. I've learned to really love myself. I had to change how I saw myself. I am not the stinky girl; I **AM** a beautiful child of the Most High God, made in His image and His likeness! **I AM ALL THAT!** He's given me a life to live. I've repented for wasting so much of it, and I now own my life and future. I am doing all that I can with my life in hopes of creating more dwelling places for Him to reside in until He comes. This is accomplished by sharing His love and allowing people to receive Jesus just as I did so He can come and dwell in them. He definitely resides in me! I'm one of His dwelling places! I want to fulfill all that He has predestined for me to accomplish. If I'm going to live with Him for all eternity, I must hear Him say, "*Well done, my good and faithful servant!*" I do **NOT** want to live with anyone for a long time and them not be pleased with me; thus, this leap of faith to share my testimony with you.

Once you receive Jesus as your Lord and Savior, you are righteous! That's the bottom line. Your spirit is new. He moves inside of you. It will take some time for the residue of the old sin nature to wither away. You may even see prior ugly behaviors rear their heads from time to time. Just know this: The new you is taking root and going way down deep. Just as He's done in my life, you, too, are going to see the new you begin to blossom. You will (for example) think, "*I should just cuss that person OUT!*", but the new spirit within you will rise up with kindness. You will then wonder, "*Was that me who thought that?*" ☺

CHAPTER THIRTEEN
God-Given Creative Ability

It is my belief that the creative power of God Almighty is within all of us. He gave each of us a measure of faith. With that measure of faith, you can use your creative ability to become and create your best 'Grace Life' ever!

"As a man thinketh, so is he." The people of Babel were building a tower to Heaven. In their minds, they could accomplish that feat. In a moment, it was as if God got up out of His seat to see what they were up to. Upon realizing their task, he confounded their language to stop the manifestation of that tower! They couldn't finish building it because they couldn't understand one another!

I am creating a world of total extravagance because I want to enjoy Heaven while on Earth (prior to my departure). If you can imagine it, it's good, and will not cause harm to anyone, I believe it can become a reality. I believe that is the creative ability God has given us and, as we mature with the use of our creative ability, more power is entrusted to us. I will finance the end-time gospel because I want to take as many people to Heaven with me as possible!

During my formative years, I really enjoyed sweets. I'd happily leave playing with friends to accompany my parents to the grocery store. While they were shopping, having meat butchered, or just perusing the aisles, I would go to the cookie aisle, open a package, and eat as many as I could before casually walking back to wherever my parents were. They would purchase other cookies...and I would eat those as well! Talk about a Cookie Monster...Lucy was it!!! My parents didn't have a clue.

Whenever we'd visit relatives, they would always take me to the kitchen and give me cookies. My grandmother would bake a chocolate frosted cake whenever she knew I was coming to visit. I was totally hooked on sugar - and it reflected in my size. I wore Chubbetts, which were similar to plus sizes today.

So, why do we introduce our children to sugar, knowing it is totally bad for their health? We know how to read labels. We know sugar has side effects. We know sugar is detrimental to our health. We know about sugar diabetes. We've even read that sugar is a breeding ground for cancer! If you never introduce your child to sugar, that is one less stronghold they will not have to conquer later in life. I never thought I would live without sweets, but deliverance came!

W.A.T.?

God tells us in His Word that we are to train up a child in the way they should go, and when they are old, they will not depart from it (Proverbs 22:6). So, if you educate them regarding the things that are harmful and unhealthy for a productive lifestyle, when they are old, they won't do those things. However, He did not mention when 'old' would come into being, so stay in faith for your children. Know that you can count on it to happen. You see, deliverance came for me approximately 15-20 years after giving my parents a really hard time. I wasted so much precious time, but deliverance did come!

Who'd A Thought Deliverance Would Come?

If you failed to bring up your children in the way they should go, do not fret! God also made provisions for you and your house. He loves us so much. His **GRACE** really is sufficient! He promised if you would get saved - believing in the Lord Jesus Christ - He would save you *and* your household (see Acts 16:31). So, get saved so you and your children can be saved...**NOW**! His goodness is outlined all throughout His Word. **GRACE**! *Amazing Grace!*

When you're hurting and in pain, it is very challenging to think or make sound decisions while going through withdrawal. I never thought I would wake up and not have to concern myself with where I would get my next fix (drugs); but deliverance came!!!

W.A.T.?

Dear Lord! When a virgin gave birth to Jesus Christ...when Moses and Aaron approached the Red Sea and it parted...when Nelson Mandela was in prison for 27 years, was freed, and became President...When Barack Obama became President of the United States...

WHO'D A THOUGHT?

CHAPTER FOURTEEN
I Thought I Lacked What Was Across the Tracks

Being in the wrong place at the wrong time can mess up your entire life, thwarting and sabotaging the perfect plan God has for you…**BUT** God can use the wrong places and situations to encourage someone else and *STILL* set you free.

Of course, I was this sweet, naïve girl from the good side of town. I found out that across the tracks, there were exciting things happening, so I ventured over to that side of town where the nightclubs were and where the ladies walked the streets. Men found me to be beautiful and would communicate as much to me without reservation. That attention was something I lacked in my family life.

I liked that side of town, but shortly after graduating from high school, I chose to go to New York to visit my brother and his family to learn about the 'Big Apple'. It was quite an adjustment. After a brief period, I had a return visit back to Clearwater, Florida and, of course, I went to the side of town where folks were being entertained - and were entertaining! LOL!

Who'd A Thought Deliverance Would Come?

The police would patrol the main street where the bars were. I recall a time they were harassing a young man walking down the street. The young man refused to comply with their requests. It was the weekend, and people were out having a good time. The police harassed the young man so badly, it provoked others in close proximity to rebel against what the police officers were doing. Bottles began to fly. I moved away from the activity to the other side of the street and watched from afar. Back-up officers came from everywhere. Some on foot ran past me (which, again, was on the opposite side of the street). As one of them ran past, he brushed up against me. We had a brief moment of eye contact. I was young and innocent at the time and thought, *"Is there going to be a riot?"*

The situation escalated. One of my male friends (who **never** gets involved in anything) from my side of town was arrested. I began making my way to the car when one of my female friends stopped me and said **VERY** distinctly, ***"Go home. Do not stop. Go straight home!"*** I agreed and proceeded to head home.

However, as I drove home and arrived in my neighborhood, I was prompted (by the influence of the devil) to stop and tell my friend's mom that he was arrested during the riot. I rang the doorbell (it was about 1:00 a.m.). She answered and, of course, was half asleep. I shared with her what happened. She asked me to come inside, wait until she got dressed, and go with her to the police station. I said I would. I was thinking it would be a five-minute trip: accompany her to the police station while she finds out what her son's status was. She found out he had yet to be brought to the station, so we sat and patiently waited for his arrival.

I Thought I Lacked What Was Across the Tracks

Finally, the officers who had been on the street that night came in with all the people they had arrested. Her son was among them. The officer I had that brief eye contact encounter with on the street pointed his finger at me and yelled, "*She was up there, too!*" All of a sudden, he and a few other officers came over, handcuffed me, and took me into custody. I was charged with a felony - and I was an innocent bystander! Wrong place, wrong time. They charged me with 'Throwing a deadly missile at an occupied police cruiser'. It was a very long battle. My folks spent money to bond me out and monies for an attorney; however, back in those days, it was fruitless to fight City Hall *(it is likely that way even today - unless you have a large bank roll)*.

The police officers were questioned on the witness stand and, of course, they lied. The judge sentenced me to six months in the county jail and two years' probation. I was shocked!

I saw some very bad things happen in that county jail - things I have never forgotten. Although I was there for only two months due to good behavior, the experience left me scarred from the warped judicial system to the perverted male prison guards that monitored the female dorms at night. During those two months, I thought deliverance would **NEVER** come!

It doesn't matter if I've been a low life. I know I don't deserve my Heavenly Father's love. Regardless to what happens, I'm still going to worship Him! I don't deserve His forgiveness. I don't deserve for Him to help me and make me all that I am today. I'm not here trying to deserve those things. I'm here because I know about His grace and mercy! I believe in **GRACE**! I don't qualify because of all the crap I've done, but that's the kind of God I worship and serve. Deserving or not, I believe He will see to those things I ask of Him!

Who'd A Thought Deliverance Would Come?

"...O woman, great is your faith! Let it be to you as you desire..."
Matthew 15:28

The Madman of Gadarenes was in a desperate situation. Onlookers who knew him possibly thought nothing could ever be different about him. It's possible that in his own mind, he thought he could never be rid of his self-tormenting and destructive lifestyle.

When in my own addictive behaviors and lifestyles that tore away at the moral fiber of my being, I, too, never thought life could be different. Those who knew me prior to straying so far away from my foundational upbringing and bore witness to the paths I traveled during the time of my being yoked with the enemy of my soul likely thought I could never return to the bright and respectful young lady I once was.

I agreed with them.

I thought there would never be *ANY* way I could remove myself from the bondage I had become so severely wrapped up and entangled in. **BUT GOD!**

He has a supernatural power known as *THE ANOINTING*, something He knew we would need. Anointing is defined as the burden-removing, yoke-destroying power of God. Any burden in your life or anything you've become yoked to - such as pornography, drug addiction, sugar addiction, shopping addiction, extortion, or whatever you've found yourself connected to that you should **NOT** be connected to - the anointing will remove the yoke from your neck and destroy its stronghold over your life. How do I know? Because it happened for me *AND* the Madman of Gadarenes in Mark 5!

W.A.T.?

I Thought I Lacked What Was Across the Tracks

"For every mountain you've brought me over; for every trial you've seen me through...for this I give you PRAISE!"

For Every Mountain as sung by Kurt Carr

CHAPTER FIFTEEN
Change Your Mind, Change Your Words, Change Your Life!

The Madman of Gadarenes got his sound mind back because he encountered Jesus. The mind can be turned back on after being destroyed, per neuroscientist Dr. Caroline Leaf, as stated in her book *Switch on Your Brain*. The Word of God can change **anything**. The brain is physically destroyed with toxic thoughts and can be reversed by thinking and speaking the Word of God. You don't have to stay stuck in any situation.

CHANGE YOUR MIND!
CHANGE YOUR WORDS!
CHANGE YOUR LIFE!

Dr. Caroline Leaf states, "*Misuse of the mind will cause our brain and body to suffer.*" Watch what you're thinking - and **DEFINITELY** watch what you're speaking. In James Allen's *As A Man Thinketh*, he shares, "*Keep your hand firmly upon the helm of thought... Right thought is mastery.*"

Thoughts are very powerful. It is vitally important to watch what you're thinking about and what you're allowing to take up space in your mind. If you activate your thought-life in a positive manner - thinking on those things that are good, pure, lovely, and of good report - your brain will flourish! What you're thinking can manifest in this natural world.

Change Your Mind, Change Your Words, Change Your Life!

It is possible to lose every physical possession you have acquired, but as long as you have a sane mind, it is possible to regain all that was lost - especially if you have the mind of Christ. He can give you wisdom and insight on how to execute ideas, concepts, and insights. He can thrust you farther ahead than you were prior to your losses.

The Madman of Gadarenes lost his mind and was living in the tombs; however, upon his encounter with Jesus, every stronghold that held him captive **HAD** to set him free. Jesus loves us so much and has great compassion for us. He didn't ask the Madman if he created the negative situation he was in. He didn't judge him. Instead, He helped the man. He restored the man. When you encounter love, you get everything you'll ever need for a productive, successful life.

After being restored, the Madman asked to follow Jesus. Many times, when a person is delivered from drug addiction, extortion, prostitution, pornography, hardened heart, or whatever it is, you will **WANT** to follow Jesus as well because of the love and compassion He delivers to you. He is not condemning. You will **WANT** to hang around Him more and more. However, as with the Madman, Jesus asks of us that we return home to let the people see what the Lord has done in your life. We are not to sit inside the church and just "hang around" Jesus. Jesus needs us to let those in our workplace, homes, and other places we frequent (such as the grocery store, beauty salon, barber shop, or wherever we go), we need to allow them to see the love of God in our lives and share with them what great things the Lord has done for us! We are Jesus' 'Marketing Department'. We need to do our jobs and share His goodness. That's the bottom line!

Who'd A Thought Deliverance Would Come?

After my deliverance from being in captivity, I felt so free and loving. I became hungry for more of that love and deliverance I had encountered. I attended church and Bible studies. I served in my church. I volunteered with an outreach ministry for teens. I wanted to share the love I had encountered with others so they, too, could experience the Great Deliverer. I preached to the children in my day care center. I preached to the children in Children's ministry. I preached to the men in the prisons as a team member of the Prison Ministry. I could not refrain from sharing the exceeding joyous life I am blessed to have!

That's what the Madman did! He went and shared his deliverance with others who were astonished at him being a new person. Life is not fun when you're being yoked to someone or something that does not care about your well-being nor has your best interest at their forefront. That could be a person or a thing. You know what I mean!

On multiple occasions, I encountered not only physical abuse, but mental abuse as well. I was treated unkindly by associates and peers, never addressing the issues at hand. As well, I had to contend with the downgrading and condescending treatment of my then-husband. No one can negatively impact you more than someone you truly love.

Change Your Mind, Change Your Words, Change Your Life!

I have been in some relationships that were very abusive. I thought they would never end. I have worked on jobs that were less than desirable. I wanted to break free, but needed the income. I have been in excruciating pain and thought I would have to live with it for the rest of my life. I have been set free from physically-abusive relationships, only to find myself in mentally-abusive ones. Check this one out (this is a scary one): I have been in churches, wanting the truth about God, and wondered if deliverance would ever come - because I was abused there, too!

W.A.T.?

I have been in debt with a mortgage - which has one definition of being in a death grip - and I spoke to the debt. I paid additional monies with each payment...and the debt seemed to increase! I have stared lack in the face and wondered time and again when it was going to leave. I began to see that although the enemy painted the picture of lack in my mind, when I *CHANGED* my mind and began to notice I always had food to eat...I always had a nice roof over my family's head...I was blessed to pay my children's tuition or provide quality home-schooling...my children always looked and dressed nice when going outside the home...we always had a car, income, and provisions were always there...when those changes in my mindset came, I began to view the glass as half-full and took notice there was **NO** lack in my life.

Remember:

> *AS A MAN THINKETH*
> *IN HIS HEART,*
> *SO IS HE.*

Who'd A Thought Deliverance Would Come?

When I began to value myself (more than I had during the abusive relationships), I no longer had to take the beatings or listen to the degrading statements and lies about myself. When I began to value myself, I didn't have to look for love in all the wrong places. I no longer needed to attempt to fill the void inside of me. It was being filled by the *ONLY ONE* who can fill it: the man I fell in love with as a young child…My Love (Jesus Christ) is mine and I am His!

Getting up every morning and going to a job I dreaded was horrific, but I had to feed my kids. When you know your worth, you're giving your best, and you're working as unto the Lord, He will deliver you. I talked to Him about it on the way into the office. While I was there, I gave my best. On my evening commute home, I talked to the Lord about it then, too. Soon, I was a part of the downsizing process. Boy, oh boy: Was I ever happy!

Deliverance may not come in the form you desire, but it always comes.

Being in bondage to drugs and having to get high every day - whether I wanted to or not - was like being yoked to the devil himself. I knew I was not raised to indulge in those activities. I knew it was wrong. I knew the people I associated with were not the best for the path on which I was supposed to be. Who you associate with is vital to your success.

Change Your Mind, Change Your Words, Change Your Life!

Waking up in the morning and having drugs on my mind first thing until I got high - then, when I got high, I had the next fix on my mind because I knew the current high would soon diminish - was a vicious cycle known as 'My Life'. That cycle continued day after day, night after night - until I desired to be set free. There was a series of events that led to my being set free. I fell back into the ditch and was pulled out again. I fell off the wagon and climbed back on again. **BUT** when *JESUS* stepped on the scene, He saw my heart's desire to be free. He delivered me and (just as He did with the Madman) made me whole!

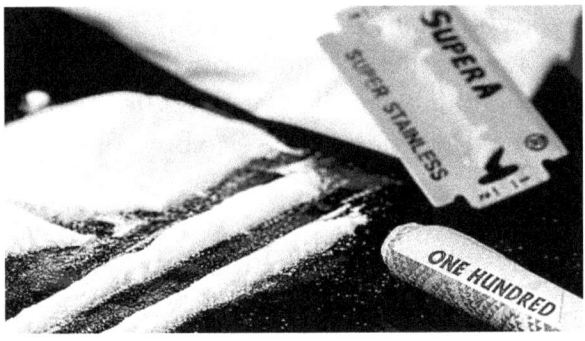

You think your children will never stop behaving in a way that is unseemly. I'm sure my parents were very displeased with the road I traveled after having been raised in a quality home and environment, but they never gave up on me. Jesus changed **MY** life! If you keep believing, your children will come up out of the ditch, too! My parents didn't know how to intercede or confess the Word like I know how to do today, but I knew Jesus and had accepted Him as a child. He was right there with me going through all of that filth and shame. The seed of the righteous shall be delivered.

Who'd A Thought Deliverance Would Come?

My own children have hurt me severely and put me through some very uncomfortable, painful experiences, but they all have told me how much they appreciate me praying for, loving, and being supportive of them - even through all of their seemingly unchanging attitudes and lifestyles. The Word of God says your children will rise up and call you **BLESSED**!

Deliverance comes! I'm telling you!

My son had asthma for years and years...and years. At one point, I just stopped giving him breathing treatments and other medications because I could see how harmful they were. I researched and found the damage that was created by those drugs. I had to stay in **FAITH FORCE** mode for his well-being. He was freed from asthma! Thank God! **FINALLY!**

It may look like there's no end in sight, but deliverance comes!

Having been arrested for a crime I did not commit and serving time in jail for said crime, I found myself wondering where God was through it all. After being released two months into a six-month sentence, I realized this: Jesus had not forgotten about me - and He hasn't forgotten you, either!

Believe it or not, deliverance has already been provided for whatever you need. When I made up my mind that enough was enough...when I began to think on God and His supernatural abilities to aid others He provided for throughout His Word...then **SURELY**, He could do it for me! *HE DID!*

Everything we need is right here, right now. We need to learn to lay hold of and receive what God has already provided.

CHAPTER SIXTEEN
Hope BEYOND Hope

Deliverance comes! Actually, it is already here! All we need is for deliverance to manifest into the natural/physical realm. This takes a measure of believing… **Hope BEYOND Hope!** Only believe (see Mark 5:36).

If you really want to be set free from any bondage or situation you've found yourself entangled in and you want to be *FREE*, you must get rid of the fear of **BEING** free. Some people do not want to be free from their abusive relationships because there is an element of codependency associated with the relationship. For example, you need a place to live or you like him (when he's nice). Maybe she is a great cook and you think you can't live without her food; however, she is too controlling. **OR** even like me, the association that accompanied the drug use - living extremely fast, most of the time in a fantasy world, the intrigue of the underground world, the business acumen of the drug lords and the negotiating skills of those addicted, eating on the go and eating out all of the time, wearing the latest fashions, the camaraderie, the attention, and the entire infatuation - it was all deceit and meant to steer me away from my purpose.

Some people don't want to be set free from illnesses (healed) because it could possibly terminate their disability payments or their free medications they so enjoy. That is only because there's the fear of the unknown of what life would be like *without* that bondage.

Who'd A Thought Deliverance Would Come?

The saying goes, "Hindsight is always 20/20" - meaning we are able to see more clearly and with understanding those things that have transpired after the fact. We often see why it happened and the way it did. As we mature and move forward, we can then share with others because we now have "20/20 vision".

As I transitioned from being in bondage, I've had to learn to forgive myself and those who inflicted pain on me - be it mental or physical. I endured a great deal of physical beatings, but I learned to get out of those relationships. I also decided to not carry all of that hurtful and painful baggage with me. I learned to say, *"No! I am not going to accompany you down that road anymore. I do forgive you, though."* It is okay to cut ties that are toxic. It is definitely okay to forgive yourself and cut out the negative self-talk. Learn to silence your inner-critic!

Confidence rarely exudes from a person who is not comfortable in his or her own skin. A minister stated years ago, *"Don't nurse it, don't rehearse it, and don't curse it."* Let by-gones be by-gones. Let sleeping dogs lie. Forget the past hurts and challenges. Let them *GO* and **FOCUS** on how you see your new, beautiful future! If you continue to talk about the hurt, you stay in that place of hurt. Let it **GO**!

My parents divorced after many years of marriage. They later reconciled, and although they got back together, my mother remained bitter for reasons unknown to me. My dad was a little envious because my mother was more successful than he. After having worked the majority of her life, my mother had reaped the benefits of retirement.

One day, she was out gardening in her flower beds and had a seizure - something she never had before. We took her to the hospital, and they gave her medication intravenously. The seizure lasted for over 12 hours. I prayed for my mother and talked to the Lord about what was going on with her. I asked Him how to best work in order to have complete healing manifest. After many tests, it was found my mother had brain cancer. There were little fingers of cancer throughout her brain and the doctors stated they should operate right away. I asked the neurosurgeon if he was of the same faith as I, and surprisingly, he said he was! My mother had the surgery, followed by radiation and chemotherapy. I found it unfortunate when the surgeon said there were too many of those 'fingers' of cancer throughout my mother's brain to remove all of the disease.

I would take her to all of her treatments and to prayer at the neighborhood church. I watched as my mother's hair came out in her comb as she would attempt to get dressed. I also noticed a significant decline in her appetite after chemotherapy and how she could not keep anything on her stomach. It was the most disheartening experience because I loved my mother. To watch her deteriorate before my eyes was extremely painful. I prayed and asked God to manifest His healing power in my mother's body. I knew Him as a Healer because He had healed me from back pains and secondary cellulitis (an infection going to my brain after being beaten in the head with the butt of a gun). God responded to my request *with* a request: He told me to ask my mother if she would forgive my father. Forgive him for what, I do not know; however, I was obedient. I went to my mother privately and told her what God said. She never said yes or no, but only shook her head from side to side in tears in response to the request. I believe her inability to genuinely forgive my father played into her critical condition.

Who'd A Thought Deliverance Would Come?

Forgiveness and our thoughts play a crucial role in how our brain functions, which, in turn, affects our physical bodies. Although my mother did not receive the *physical* manifestation of her healing, she did receive her deliverance from the torment of cancer eating away at her brain. I firmly believe the debilitating condition of the cancer was a direct result of the tormenting thoughts and unforgiveness she harbored for a long time. Her deliverance came in the form of her real person - her spirit - being set free through death; death being separation from the physical body and being united with the Creator.

My brother had moved into my mother's home because her sisters and her mother came and took her back to her hometown to live with them for a while. My father relocated there as well. My brother had no car at the time, so I would pick him up every morning to give him a ride to work on my way into the office. I would pull up in the driveway, and sometimes he would come right out. Other times, I would have to blow the horn. On this one particular morning, he came to the door and beckoned for me to come inside. I told him I didn't have the time and that we had to go. He was insistent that I come inside…for just a moment.

I climbed out of the car and, as I approached him, I could see his countenance was very sad. I stepped inside the door and he immediately informed me our mother had passed away. I dropped to the floor to my knees and began worshipping God. Tears were streaming down my face as I blessed, worshipped, and thanked Him for allowing my mother to be released from all of her pain and agony. She had gotten to the point where she could not talk, walk, or do anything for herself. All she was able to do was peer out through her beautiful eyes. That in itself had to be agonizing...

I continued crying and worshipping God and thanked Him for giving me such a wonderful mother. I prayed earnestly for her while she was away living with our relatives. I was so certain she would come back home one day, but it didn't quite work out that way. Still...her **DELIVERANCE** came!

W.A.T.?

As I worshipped on the floor of my parents' home and thanked God for receiving my mother into Heaven, I felt good about her temporary separation from me in this Earth because I have hope, knowing I will see her again (see 1 Thessalonians 4:13). Mother's deliverance came! Not how I expected it to come, but my expectation did not halt her deliverance! She is no longer in agony. She is in Heaven seeing beauty that far exceeds anything she had ever known. She is experiencing divine health and extraordinary, unconditional love like never before. She is having the time of her life - and it's taking place for all of eternity. I'm so excited knowing I **WILL** see her again!

Who'd A Thought Deliverance Would Come?

Reflecting back on Mark Chapter Five: There was a man named Jairus whose *daughter* was sick (a complete reversal of my situation). I sought Jesus to heal my mother, and Jairus sought Jesus to heal his child. Jairus sought the One who could heal his child, and assuredly, that was Jesus. Jesus - being the loving, willing person He is - began to walk with Jairus to his home in order to heal his daughter. While headed in that direction, a woman with an illness of hemorrhaging forced her way to Jesus and touched His clothing. Her deliverance came that day. She had taken a serious risk by coming outside in her condition, but sometimes when you are desperate, you have to take risks and do something you've never done before. She believed, acted, and received deliverance from her disease (see Mark 5:23); however, in the meantime, she had created a distraction from Jesus getting to Jairus' daughter who was lying at the point of death.

The distraction with the woman getting her healing from Jesus seemingly took an amount of time - so much so that one of the people from Jairus' house came to tell him his daughter had already died and that he shouldn't trouble Jesus anymore. Upon hearing the message, Jesus immediately turned to Jairus and said, *"FEAR NOT! ONLY BELIEVE!"* When you're with the One who has all power, you cannot entertain fear. Fear will cancel out what you are believing God for.

Fear has an acronym that spells out:

F = False
E = Evidence
A = Appearing
R = Real

You must learn to **ONLY BELIEVE!** In the midst of a bad report, keep on believing. Do *NOT* entertain fear.

Hope BEYOND Hope

When Jairus received the report that his daughter was already dead, he could have gotten mad at Jesus and said, "*If you hadn't taken so much time with that woman who was hemorrhaging, maybe you would have made it to my daughter in time.*" Instead, Jairus kept his mouth closed and did as Jesus instructed. He did not fear. He kept right on believing. When they finally arrived at Jairus' home, folks were already mourning his daughter's death.

In the midst of you believing for God to do something for you, you will sometimes be faced with opposition. People will tell you it's too late and that it's over! **NO!** It's not over until *JESUS* says it's over.

In Mark 5:40, Jesus put all of those mourners out of Jairus' house, then went in to minister to Jairus' daughter.

Sometimes, you have to put some people out of your life. Get rid of everyone who is not supporting your vision. Get rid of the naysayers. Get rid of the **DREAM KILLERS**. You can get rid of people by distancing yourself from them. You can get rid of people by cutting them off completely and having nothing else to do with them. With others, you may choose to continue in a safe proximity with them, but no longer discuss your dreams - and shut them *down* if they attempt to bring your dreams and goals up in **their** conversation. You cannot reach your goals if you have someone pulling you down two rungs on the ladder of success each time you climb one rung!

Back to the story: Jesus put them **OUT!** He was there to take care of business. Bringing Jairus' daughter back to life required faith. Faith operates better in an environment that is conducive for miracles. One of doubt and unbelief could be a hindrance. The mourners were laughing at Jesus - and He put them **OUT!**

Who'd A Thought Deliverance Would Come?

Although Jesus had been distracted by the woman with the issue of blood…although Jairus' daughter had died…timing is not a challenge for Jesus. He is the real deal - and He successfully completed the mission at hand. Jairus' daughter LIVED AGAIN! Her deliverance came! It didn't look like it with all that had transpired, but remember: We are to **NOT** be moved by our senses, which includes those things we see with our naked eyes. We **ARE** to be moved by what God promised us in His Word.

I recall being on a conference call with John Maxwell one morning. During the call, he spoke of being invited back to a church to minister - a church in a city where people from his past still resided. He was invited to lunch with one of his old buddies. He said after they shared stories from past experiences, they had nothing more to talk about. John had obviously outgrown his old friend and, after ministering, there was nothing to hold him there to visit any longer.

Sometimes, people are in your life for a season. It is unhealthy to force or foster a relationship when its natural end has come. Terminate it! Learn to let go of the past and look forward to your future. See what is unseen!

If you're being challenged with seeing a great future for yourself, spend time reading books of successful and inspirational people. A few who might interest you are: Creflo Dollar, Kenneth Copeland, Steve Harvey, Tommy Barnett, T.D. Jakes, Joel Osteen, Jim Collins, Joseph Prince, Steve Jobs, or use an inspiring daily devotional such as *Simple Abundance* by Sarah Ban Breathnach. Once you get anchored in Christ, expand your repertoire by reading books by great men; however, be mindful always to "chew up the fish and spit out the bones".

Hope BEYOND Hope

In Steve Harvey's book, *Act Like a Success; Think Like a Success*, he helps readers locate their gift/calling they have inside. He goes on to encourage us to master our fears and to keep trying new careers or attain new goals that will possibly catapult us into greatness.

Kenneth Copeland's book, *The Blessing of the Lord*, gives insight on how to operate in our covenant with God. We have rights to certain things. We need not be ignorant of what belongs to us. If someone has an inheritance for us and we don't know how to acquire it, we are still in the same predicament we were in prior to knowing and claiming that inheritance!

In his book, *8 Steps to Create the Life You Want; The Anatomy of a Successful Life*, Creflo Dollar teaches that we must be aware of our mindsets and habits because they play a big part in character development - which ultimately leads us to our destination.

These wonderful authors help us get the kind of picture of ourselves that we want to hold on to and use to manifest our hearts' desires!

Joel Osteen's book, *Break Out*, encourages us to go beyond the barriers that have held us where we are and to stay with it until we see the vision we have for ourselves come to fruition.

Many start the transformation; however, some fall by the wayside. **YOU**, my friend, *MUST* learn to stay in the game! I have witnessed sporting games that appeared to be over…a loss…a wipeout. Just as quickly as I could blink, the tables turned and the team that I had thought **SURELY** lost the game actually came back and **WON**! Learn to never quit. Stay in the game!

Who'd A Thought Deliverance Would Come?

Authors like Lisa Nichols are phenomenal, coming from (as she says) South Central Los Angeles. She paints a picture of that area being the survival of the fittest! Lisa speaks in her book about moving from being angry to taking *ACTION*. Doing something about our situations to change them is a way to redirect the anger energy that will thrust our whining and complaining into stepping out and up into a new life.

Once you've read others' successful endeavors, you can close your eyes and see yourself doing some great things. Your ability to dream can be the entryway into your future. Use your imagination for something spectacular! In Genesis 11:6, the Lord said, "*...nothing will be restrained from them that they have imagined to do.*" I say to myself (as I use my imagination to create a desired world of being able to bless millions and millions of people and to live a life of Heaven on Earth), I say, "**LUCY, nothing will be restrained from you that you've imagined to do.**"

> *IMAGINATION: THE PREVIEW TO LIFE'S COMING ATTRACTIONS.*

See, if you are going to create a lifestyle of happiness and success, you will need to read books *AND* go to church. I go to church and I get seed (exemplary teachings) from my Pastor. I then plant that seed in my heart and speak it out of my mouth. I also teach myself at home. I execute what I am taught and go back to get more seed. I continue to plant it in my heart and it continues to deliver harvest after harvest.

I am not the same person I was 30 years ago, 20 years ago, 10 years ago, or even just last year. I continue to learn and grow. I read enumerable books on faith, success, business, and the mind.

Dr. Caroline Leaf has an exceptional teaching entitled *Who Turned Off My Brain*. She brings the connection to the forefront on how our thoughts influence our brains. It is **HIGHLY** recommended that you read her book!

We live in an information age. There is too much information at our fingertips for us not to be successful and do something with the talent **GOD** gave us. Do not be fearful of being successful!

Who'd A Thought Deliverance Would Come?

Marianne Williamson stated it very clearly in an excerpt from her book *Return to Love*:

Our Deepest Fear

Our deepest fear is not that we are inadequate.

Our deepest fear is that we are powerful beyond measure.

It is our light, not our darkness, that most frightens us.

We ask ourselves, "Who am I to be brilliant, gorgeous, handsome, talented, and fabulous?"

Actually, who are you not to be?

You are a child of God.

Your playing small does not serve the world.

There is nothing enlightened about shrinking so that other people won't feel insecure around you.

We are all meant to shine, as children do.

We were born to make manifest the glory of God within us.

It is not just in some; it is in everyone.

And, as we let our own light shine, we consciously give other people permission to do the same.

As we are liberated from our fear, our presence automatically liberates others.

CHAPTER SEVENTEEN
If Not You, Then Who?

As you choose to step out and fulfill your purpose in life, you give others around you the motivation and green light to go ahead and do what **THEY** were created to do.

It is my belief that we are all interconnected. Each of us has something that is needed by someone else that only we can give. As we do what we are destined to do, it satisfies a need in someone's life - someone who has been waiting for what you and *ONLY* you can give.

The questions, then, are:

If not you, then who? If not now, then WHEN?

For about 20 years, I was reluctant to complete this book because of the guilt and shame associated with my past. I didn't want to lay my soul bare before the world and allow everyone to see I had serious flaws, along with a scarred and marred past. I had to step across that threshold and allow my past, brokenness, pain, and abuse to become visible to the world because people are walking around hurting. They don't know how they will get through tomorrow.

I'm here to tell you:

DELIVERANCE COMES!

It's going to be okay!

Who'd A Thought Deliverance Would Come?

Let's look at an abbreviated list of things I have encountered along life's journey:

- Multiple physical beatings, including being pistol-whipped (beaten in my head with a gun)
- Drug abuse
- Rejection
- Lack
- Depression and attempted suicide
- Being Fat - sugar addiction
- Falsely accused, convicted, and jailed
- Evicted while being a single mother with three children
- Holidays and birthdays with minimal ability to honor and celebrate my children
- Being talked about in the church - the one place I loved because of the refuge it afforded from all the hurt and pain the world dished out…and because I love God and His people

GOD brought forth deliverance from each and every one of the aforementioned situations! I believe He did it so I could share the gory details with you in order for you to know beyond a shadow of a doubt that regardless of how hard you are blindsided (struck and caught off-guard with tragedy or disappointment), there **IS** a way out. He promised to make a way in the wilderness and rivers in the desert - and He reminded me of that at one of my lowest points (see Isaiah 43:19). You see, if He didn't deliver me out of each of those challenging circumstances, I'd be able to refer to Him as a "DBD" (Dead-Beat Dad). He is **NOT** that kind of Father at all! He *always* provides a way of escape. He loves His children, and just as I love my children through good times and not-so-good times, God truly loves us…**HIS** children (see Matthew 7:11).

If Not You, Then Who?

Learn to love yourself. That was something I had never been taught nor told. My parents were not very affectionate. I don't recall ever being told by them that they loved me...

Let me break right here and tell you something: If your parents never told you they loved you, *THEIR* parents probably never told them. We usually model behaviors we have seen. I speak for my parents and your parents: If they never showed you affection, they did the best they could. Now, it's up to us to change that and communicate love and affection to our children, as we now know how vital doing so is to their well-being and overall success.

Growing up, I was **so** chubby. I was not told I was loved and valuable - even after I later lost weight and was very attractive. No one validated me, so the first man who gave me some attention, I fell for the trickery and smooth lines.

SIDEBAR: If no one validates you, you get in that mirror and validate yourself!

Men should do it, too! You need to know you're valuable and successful. You need to know you're very good-looking and you have what it takes to be **GREAT**!

An analogy I use with my children regarding their worth includes the jewelry story. I share with them the following:

As you enter Neiman Marcus, Harrod's, or any other store that sells jewelry, there are pieces in the aisles on display tables that any and every one can fondle, touch, and tamper with as they walk by. That jewelry catches their eye - and they can even try pieces on to decide whether or not they would like to purchase it. Those pieces are *costume* jewelry.

Who'd A Thought Deliverance Would Come?

Then there's the designer jewelry behind the counter in the locked case. Those pieces, the sales associate would have to retrieve with the use of a key to unlock the cabinet in order for you to have an up-close and personal look at them. This jewelry is a little better quality than that of the jewelry on display in the aisles; however, the sales associate will give the jewelry to you - although it has been locked up - and allow you to touch and examine it in order for you to make a decision about purchasing and taking it home with you. Those pieces are *designer* jewelry.

I'm sure by now, you're getting the picture...

We now make an **appointment** to examine diamonds at a fine jeweler's location. Once the appointment is made and our desires have been expressed to the jeweler, we can rest assured - knowing we will view untouched and untampered *PURE* products. You share with the jeweler what it is you're hoping to find. You don't touch anything! Diamonds are such an awesome creation from God with a WOW-factor built in. They have beauty that is intriguing with an expressive way of desiring to be touched; however, jewelers do **NOT** allow potential clients to touch their fine jewels because of the grime and unseen oils from your fingertips that could tarnish the natural beauty of the diamond. The jeweler will even wear gloves and use tweezers to pick up the diamond to allow you to see it on a velvet cloth that reflects its natural beauty. To examine it more closely, you can view it through a small telescope. Diamonds sparkle and shine. Everyone stares at a beautiful diamond because it screams very loudly: **I AM BEAUTIFUL! I AM UNTOUCHED! I AM CLEAN!** Those pieces are *precious stones* jewelry.

If Not You, Then Who?

I wanted both of my daughters *AND* my son to know how valuable they are and how important it is not to be tainted by the world's way of living, thinking, and being. I encouraged them to take time to remain invaluable by realizing their self-worth and true value. I gave each of them a diamond ring and shared with them the importance of maintaining their virginity.

As I came into the knowledge of valuing myself, I passed that information on to my children. If children are never taught, how do you expect them to know how to live properly? Even if they stumble and stray, you have made rich deposits that will be with them to help them come back to their original location.

"Penthouse Living"

Repent means to return to the high place. Get up from your fallen state and get back up to where you belong. You are a child of the **KING**! You are Kings and Priests. You are Queens, Princes, and Princesses…Royal Priesthood! What in the heck are you doing remaining in despair when you are **ROYALTY**?

REPENT! Turn away from the thing that you've done that is not of your character. Royalty doesn't allow every Tom, Dick, Harry, Susie, and Jane to touch them. If (by some *REMOTE* chance) **ROYALTY** gets tainted, failure and remaining in a slump is not an option.

REPENT! 'Re' meaning *GO BACK*! 'Pent' meaning *HIGHEST PLACE*! Return to the high place and receive the deliverance that has already been made available to you. Receive it. Take it. Apply it. Move on to greater success and victory. With deliverance always coming for you, you can fall down - but remember to get back up again!

Who'd A Thought Deliverance Would Come?

Also note the following: Your life's plans may not be the same as your best buddy, so don't throw shade (act in an unseemly, dislike manner towards another; jealousy, etc.) at someone because they are more successful than you. Use that unseemly energy by directing it towards yourself and turning inward to find out what it is you are supposed to be doing to make life better - not only for yourself, but for someone else.

We have gifts and talents given to us so that we can be a light to someone in darkness. You must receive your deliverance because someone is waiting on you. You have what they need to help them make it on the remaining portion of the journey.

I am writing to let you know you can make it through the storms of life. I am sharing to let you know deliverance **WILL** come for you.

You are here to share your light in order to let others who are 'waiting' on you know what it is that you need to share with them in order for their light to be ignited **AND** in order for them to be the helping hand others in their own circle of influence need.

CHAPTER EIGHTEEN
We ARE Our Brother's Keeper

We go through different experiences in our lives for multiple reasons. Keeping those experiences locked away inside will not help others make it to where they need to go, be, or do.

An old African proverb shared by a storyteller once stated, *"The mouth should be open wide to let what is inside come out."* Two things can happen:

1. The person who allows whatever it is that is inside that needs to be released gets free when the release is made; and/or
2. The person listening to what is being released gains insight on how to be free/delivered or possibly share the information with someone they know who could benefit.

It is **SO** amazing how we are all interconnected and play a major role in each other's success!

We actually **ARE** our brother's keeper!

The Madman of Gadarenes encountered Jesus, received what Jesus said, and had deliverance manifested in his life. He went to spread the word about what happened to him - and others received what they needed from him and his message. That could have been hope someone needed. Maybe another heard about the Deliverer and, like Doubting Thomas (see John 20), needed to actually **SEE** the manifestation - and the Madman provided the proof that person needed.

Who'd A Thought Deliverance Would Come?

What about you? Maybe you feel as if you do not need deliverance today. Maybe you are not locked in an addictive behavior. Maybe you're not the one extorting money from your company. Perhaps it's possible that the sugar demon lures you into its web and grips you with its ugly talons. Whatever it is that you no longer want to do (or know you should not do), know this: Deliverance awaits you!

Take a look at the 'real' you. Whatever needs to be changed or removed can be! Sarah Ban Breathnach remarks in her *Simple Abundance: A Daybook of Comfort and Joy*, "Some of us have remained dormant for years - oblivious to our genuine beauty - drugged senseless by our own numbing disapproval, nagging doubts, and benign neglect. Coping strategies that once brought a sense of relief now only offer regret. To undo the damage and reconnect with our authentic selves, we need to take the plunge, confident that the Spirit is holding the net. Above all, we need to treat ourselves gently with the kindness we would bestow on amnesiacs who need the patient reassurance of their true identities."

For many years, the Madman of Gadarenes possibly felt he was foreign to himself - living in the tombs with the dead, cutting himself, not knowing he was fearfully and wonderfully made. I, too, found myself numbing myself with drugs, feeling unlovely and unloved. I "lived" in the symbolic tombs, being associated with those who had no direction nor respect for their lives. We were inflicting ourselves with hurtful narcotics, never thinking beyond the next high. Some of my associates died in those "tombs", never experiencing their true, beautiful self…always accepting the lies of the enemy of our soul about who they were not!

We ARE Our Brother's Keeper

Deliverance came for them, but they were too afraid to see their inner-beauty…too afraid to implore their many strengths in order to soar…too afraid to be beautiful…too afraid to be successful…too afraid to break free from the enemy's fatal talons and traps.

As a child, nobody ever told me they **loved** me. As a result, I sought to fill that void wherever I could. Yes, I was told I was smart. Yes, I was told I could do well in life. Those things did not compensate for the lack of love and validation that I was great just the way I was. I always saw myself as the outcast: fat and unattractive. Any minute promise of love was well-received and, unfortunately, compensated for in negative ways.

I now know how to celebrate, validate, and give accolades to myself. I know how to reward me! I don't wait to be celebrated anymore. I know how to ask God to celebrate me and I know how to purchase for myself experiences that I enjoy and items that make me feel good about who I am *AND* my surroundings. Yeah! I know how to and enjoy doing motivational self-talk! I know how to protect my environment and steer clear of those who speak guile…those evil speakers, gossipers, and negative talkers! I like thinking grandioso thoughts. **I LOVE BEING HAPPY AND POSITIVE!** That's who I am now! I'm all that! My name is *LUCY TODD!*

CHAPTER NINETEEN
It's Not Too Late to Begin Anew

RITUALS

Being a druggie is such a selfish life. You think of feeding the monkey on your back and very little else...but there are rituals associated with getting high.

Rituals are defined by Dictionary.com as "prescribed, established, or ceremonial acts or features collectively, as in religious services".

In the process of smoking marijuana or intravenously injecting heroin or cocaine in your veins, the people you find yourself engaged with in the shooting galleries or smoke houses all perform their specific rituals in the process of preparing the drugs for intake.

You may have begun the ritual prior to coming together to get high, shucking and jiving about how you were able to make your monies for your drugs during that day - or maybe you're in the corporate world and you smoke a nice Cuban cigar as you and your business partner discuss your successful takeover of a competitor's firm that you've long awaited to take down. Maybe prior to lovemaking, you may enjoy foreplay or even a little Jack Daniels, Hennessey, smooth jazz, or R&B to get you in the mood.

It's Not Too Late to Begin Anew

John Maxwell once spoke at a church in which I was a member in Tampa, Florida many years ago. While there, he ran a parallel between the corporate businessman and the drug dealer. Both do an enormous amount of business, marketing, selling, looking for new opportunities, etc. However, the drug dealer was not afforded the same opportunities as the businessman, although his hustle, drive, and business acumen was just as dedicated as that of his counterpart.

Back to rituals...

Rituals - in whatever form - are addictive. They carry with them an association, usually attached to something enjoyable. Thus, drug addiction is not the only addictive behavior to be broken or destroyed. New environments to replace the hustle mindset must be implemented for the delivered addict. Whenever doing away with an unhealthy eating disorder or alcohol stronghold, one must deny himself or herself the addictive product while simultaneously renewing one's mind to new, healthy patterns.

Too many times to mention, I've quit smoking, quit drugs, and quit eating sugar, only to find myself binging on them once again. Letting go of gambling is fine; however, the rituals, fun trips, and casinos carry with them their pull on you as well. The inner *AND* the outer must change.

Dr. Caroline Leaf shares in her book, *Think and Eat Yourself Smart*, the following: "We literally have to convince our dominant, nonconscious level of mind by building an automatized, reconceptualized mindset into, which replaces the reason we have an unhealthy diet, and unhealthy weight in the first place...the toxic behaviors of our pasts do not have to take over our future. We are what we think."

Who'd A Thought Deliverance Would Come?

Here's food for thought: You are what the animal you're eating ate! If you're eating pork, you're eating what the pig ate because what he ate is in his cells, etc.

Once you're engaged in your productive, new life, there's the business of doing business. The first order of business is **YOURSELF...YOUR LIFE!**

Establish order! Begin again with a new ritual...one that promises success. Get involved in church regularly and ongoing. Just as you're learning to exercise, eat right, and take better care of your physical body, become aware of the real person who resides inside of your skin. That's **YOU!** Restructure your life. Receive Christ as your Lord and Savior. If you have not done so yet, you can do it right now - right where you are reading this book!

SALVATION PRAYER:

Heavenly Father, in the name of Jesus. Your Word says, *"Whosoever shall call on the name of the Lord shall be saved"* (Acts 2:21). I call to you. I ask Jesus to come into my heart and be Lord over my life according to Romans 10:9-10: *"If thou shalt confess with thy mouth the Lord Jesus, and shalt believe in thing heart that God hath raised Him from the dead, thou shalt be saved. For with the heart, man believeth unto righteousness; and with the mouth, confession is made unto salvation."* I confess that Jesus is Lord and believe in my heart that God raised Him from the dead. I am now born again. I am now a Christian and I am saved and righteous.

If you prayed that prayer, it doesn't stop there. That is just the beginning!

It's Not Too Late to Begin Anew

With your new life, you have been afforded gifts and talents. You are to utilize those gifts and talents as God directs. You are to do business with the gifts you have. You are to occupy until He comes back for us. We are here to fulfill a divine purpose, and your job is to find out what that purpose is and **GO FOR IT** with all you have!

The drugs, alcohol, eating disorders, and unhealthy sexual cravings were all distractions along the road to deter you from doing what you were designed to do in this world.

Let me share with you some of my struggles on the path to the good life I now live…

STRUGGLES

Drugs. Low self-esteem. Not having love communicated to me as a child. Being told I was unworthy. Made to feel devalued because of some ignorant people needing to make themselves feel an inflated sense of value. Having the family doctor prescribe Valium for me in high school for menstrual cycle irregularity. Being overweight as a child. Being called "Oreo" because of White acquaintances. Playing mom and dad with friends and being pitched in the dad role. Having my dad tell me over and over again that when I was born and the doctor delivered me in our home, he handed me right back to the doctor and said, "*She should have been a boy*".

Of course, the list of struggles could continue, but I want you to know this: Regardless of what your list entails - whether they're in the personal or business arena - there's an end to them.

DELIVERANCE COMES!

Who'd A Thought Deliverance Would Come?

Many times, we are a product of our environment without giving much attention to the incubator we're being formed in. Our thoughts, decisions, actions, and mannerisms are indelibly engrained in us, shaping our character and being.

My mother held a management position long before Blacks were "qualified" to do so. My father served in the military. My mother was more regimented than my father in her home life, and I later learned (when I became employed by her) that she was just as strict "on the job", exhibiting a perfectionist drive.

I adopted many of my parents' rigid traits. I became a drill sergeant to my children...not their mother. Simply put: I became what I saw modeled in my home as I grew up. I never saw affection being shared between my parents openly; neither did my parents ever tell me they loved me. I was never told I was beautiful; neither did they verbalize they were proud of my excellent grades. They didn't praise me for any of my many clarinet, upright bass, singing, or acting performances; neither did they take special notice of my profound Easter and Christmas speeches that were carefully memorized and articulated with perfection. You know what? That's okay, because I've now learned to tell **MYSELF** how much I am loved by my Heavenly Father - and I tell my children every time I talk to them that **I LOVE THEM!**

It's Not Too Late to Begin Anew

I remember having a conversation with my father about my future goals and desires. I said, "*Dad, I desire to be a recording artist.*" (At the time, while watching the Ed Sullivan show on our black and white TV, that was the only place I saw successful Blacks when I was a child. It was so rare, however, I got an image of becoming a singer.) I sang in the choir at my church and my childhood friend and I would enter contests and sing. I would sing after football games at McDonald's for my Caucasian friends who would encourage me to sing. A little later in life, I would sing at Piano Bars while being accompanied by the piano player.

(My parents were not aware - reason being my dad told me I needed to go to college and get a career that could provide stability. He crushed my dream of becoming a recording artist…)

Although I have yet to become a recording artist - and please remember always that God's plan for your life will prevail - I have used my lovely voice as a voiceover talent for commercials, announcements, training, teaching, and preaching. So, I guess I **CAN** be referred to as a 'Recording Talent'! ☺

Muhammad Ali was quoted as saying, "*The man who has no imagination has no wings.*" That is such a profound statement, and if you meditate on it, you may come to realize why you're not soaring.

James Allen gave birth to a prolific, great read entitled *As a Man Thinketh*, which is an off-shoot of Proverbs 23:7 from the King James Version of the Bible. What you focus on, you have the potential to become. What you say has the potential to come to pass.

Who'd A Thought Deliverance Would Come?

We've been given an imagination to use for unimaginable blessings - not for the enemy to get in your mind with his filth and trash. Begin sitting for five minutes a day with no distractions and just **THINK**. *Think* of being the one to house all the homeless people in the Winter. *Think* of providing shelter to children who desire to get out of sex trafficking. *Think* of owning some of the major buildings in your town. *Think* of having the cure for cancer and not withholding it. *Think* of living large because you're supercharged. *Think* of being able to provide vehicles for all of the single mothers in the world who need transportation. *Think* of owning the finest universities in the country and being able to hire the best teachers from around the globe. *Think* of being able to pay the United States national debt.

During the 19th century, Walter D. Wintle wrote "Thinking". Way back then, men realized the importance of thinking. We have distractions today coming at us from all angles, with only a few of us taking time to **THINK**!

Following is Wintle's poem, "Thinking".

It's Not Too Late to Begin Anew

Thinking

If you think you are beaten, you are.
If you think you dare not, you don't.
If you like to win, but you think you can't,
It is almost certain you won't.

If you think you'll lose, you're lost.
For out of the world, we find
Success begins with a fellow's will.
It's all in the state of mind.

If you think you are outclassed, you are.
You've got to think high to rise.
You've got to be sure of yourself before
You can ever win a prize.

Life's battles don't always go
To the stronger or faster man;
But sooner or later, the man who wins
Is the man WHO THINKS HE CAN!

~ By Walter D. Wintle ~

CHAPTER TWENTY
Learn to Dream BIGGER!

What are you thinking about yourself? *As a man thinketh in his heart, so is he.* If you're going to think about yourself, why not magnify it to a grandiose status? You are, after all, made in the image and likeness of **GOD** - and ain't *NOTHING* about Him small!

LEARN TO DREAM BIGGER!

W.A.T.?

Although I allowed my life to take a turn that led me to drugs, alcohol - and I'll even take responsibility for the prescription Valium my doctor prescribed for me as a teen - I began to think of myself in the way I wanted my life to be redirected. I knew I was greater than the way my life was heading; however, that was a product of having known I was capable of doing more while expecting more of myself than settling for being a druggie. I **THOUGHT** I could be more.

Again: What are you thinking about *YOU*?

Are you thinking you'll be where you are all of your life? If so, then guess what? You will be! If you're thinking you'll be a great, successful, well-known business owner in the future, the very seed of that thought has the potential to catapult you into that image as your reality!

The cycle of drug abuse was like being on a merry-go-round with the devil pushing it faster and faster. Round and round I went, fearful of hopping off because of the vicious cycle I found myself in. The question loomed overhead: What *ELSE* am I capable of doing?

Learn to Dream BIGGER!

I wanted more. However, I did not know how to jump off the merry-go-round of the revolving cycle of pursuing that long, sought after "high"…that high that allowed me to escape everything and everyone for a short time. I didn't know how to make new friends. My college friends treated me as if I was plagued with some disease - and they had every right to treat me that way! I didn't know how to stop the deadly cycle and get on to a **LIFE** cycle…a **PRODUCTIVE** cycle…a **BLESSED** cycle…a **FULFILLING MY PURPOSE** cycle!

GOD knew how to get me off of the spinning, out-of-control merry-go-round that Satan had me reeling and rocking on. He didn't send me to jail to get me off of drugs. Instead, He led me to a local drug rehabilitation center - one I drove myself to - and I asked them how I could get help. I was told I would live in the center and could not leave. I then inquired about how long I'd have to stay. Their response was, "*Six months to a year.*" (All I heard was 'six months'. I was **IN**!) I was in that program for approximately 18 months - a *LOT* longer than I anticipated. There was no fence. No guards. It was a fairly decent rehabilitation facility right in the heart of town - not out in the countryside or the beach.

I was required to attend group therapy meetings on a regular basis in the treatment center. While there, I enjoyed arts and crafts and indulged in physical activity. I lived in a dorm with several other women and actually made friends with some of them. The men in the program lived in a dorm across the yard. We enjoyed co-op field trips and learning activities. The latter part of the program prepared us for re-entry into society, secure employment, and (eventually) move out into our own homes.

Who'd A Thought Deliverance Would Come?

The program was a great help; however, the **MOMENT** I had a challenge, I turned to what was familiar to help me escape the present hardship. I later learned I can't win spiritual battles with physical weapons. I found total deliverance **ONLY** in Christ!

I returned to what and who I knew would forever sustain me: Jesus Christ. My sister invited me to start going back to church. She basically held my hand and kept me close to ensure I was victorious. I am so thankful for my sister because if she didn't care, I would not be a victor today.

After getting back into the groove of going to church and feeding my hungry, dry spirit, I found supplemental sources to strengthen me during the days leading up to Sunday. I'd attend home fellowship Bible studies and watch old videos of Kenneth Hagin, T.L. Osborne, and John Osteen. The home group facilitator would loan books and videos for us to take home with the promise to return them the following week for others to use. My soul and spirit were so hungry and thirsty for something new, I developed tunnel vision and focused only on learning more and more about God.

The Bible talks about renewing your mind (see Romans 12:2), which is what I was doing unaware. To become someone different, you must begin to think differently. You have to 'change the software'. Change what you think about, starve debilitating behavior, and it *WILL* die. This strategy for deliverance is not only for drug addiction. Try starving pornography (for example). Watch that monkey **LEAP** off of your back!

STARVE that desire to have sex outside of the holy bonds of matrimony.

STARVE the desire for multiple sex partners.

Learn to Dream BIGGER!

STARVE that workaholic monster that keeps you away from your children and spouse.

STARVE the gluttony demon with healthy choices.

STARVE unforgiveness and replace it with forgiveness. Be set free!

STARVE greed and power.

DELIVERANCE COMES!

Peace and pleasure on a whole new level await you. Replace the old with the new. Find new areas of life that await you. Experience something you never experienced before by starving gossip!

As deliverance came into my life from the monstrous yoke of drug addiction, I began enjoying things in life I never focused my attention on previously. My challenge to you is to allow deliverance to come in your life. **STARVE** that thing that's holding you back from where you know you deserve to be! The *POWER* is in **YOU** to do it! **JUST DO IT!**

Once deliverance came, I began to think, "*I can now have fellowship with godly men - not the guys in the drug scene.*" There were some hurdles to overcome because at that juncture, I was thinking differently about myself. Although some of the guys I met were 'supposedly' in Christ, they were on a mission: to get into my pants. I stayed focused and valued myself a great deal more than I had while living my old life of an addict. I am now a new creature in Christ (see 2 Corinthians 5:17), and all of those old things are passed away; behold, all things are become new! I now see myself in a new light!

Who'd A Thought Deliverance Would Come?

I thought I could help other people and began to volunteer as a Counselor with a renown outreach ministry for teens. I'm actively involved in church. I'm a mother to my children. I volunteer with the teens and work a full-time job. I've been clean - free from drugs - for a few years at this point and I thought to myself, "*I need a dad for my children.*" I didn't go looking; however, in my activities, I met an awesome man. He was a Corporate Executive with a Fortune 500 company - and he asked me to marry him! I shared with him 'surface' things regarding my past, but never **ALL** the gory details of how hellbound I really was.

Life was perfect for a very short time. I conceived my third child with my husband, only to have him file for a divorce. I was never told why outside of the norm: "Irreconcilable Differences". I am sure someone made him aware of my past; however, we **ALL** have a past… I lived through that heart-wrenching event. Having an additional child to care for and **NO** father for any of my children, I leaned heavily on the Lord - and I **SURVIVED**. I *THOUGHT* I could make it through…and I did!

W.A.T.?

Poems like this one penned by Maya Angelou infused strength during those seasons of the 'lowest of lows'…

Learn to Dream BIGGER!

Still I Rise! By Maya Angelou

You may write me down in history
With your bitter, twisted lies.
You may trod me in the very dirt,
But still, like dust, I'll rise.

Does my sassiness upset you?
Why are you beset with gloom?
'Cause I walk like I've got oil wells
Pumping in my living room.

Just like moons and like suns,
With the certainty of tides,
Just like hopes springing high,
Still I'll rise.

I encountered challenge after challenge with daycare providers being negligent with my third child. I decided to leave Corporate America and opened my own daycare. I actually **THOUGHT** I could run a successful business - and I did! I had people on waiting lists ready to place their children in my care. I continue to enjoy children today. Their minds are intriguing and their thoughts are pure. Their physical energies must be directed properly or they will be into everything all of the time. Their hearts and minds are tender and capable of being shaped with love, purpose, and unlimited creativity.

In comes the Lord, calling me to a new land - just as He did with Abram (see Genesis 12:1). He tugged at my heart to relocate for about a year. I finally followed His lead and, after many garage sales and prayer requests, my two youngest children helped pack up a truck with our car hitched to the back and we made the move to Atlanta, Georgia.

NO GPS. **NO** job. **NO** secured housing. *ONLY* $500.00 cash.

Who'd A Thought Deliverance Would Come?

God called me to Atlanta, so I followed His lead. **HE** provided our own housing. **HE** provided food. **HE** provided Christian schools with free tuition for *BOTH* children. **HE** provided jobs. **HE IS JEHOVAH JIREH!** I once heard Dr. Leroy Thompson refer to our Heavenly Father as a *SPONSOR*! Just think: When you have a sponsor for an event or project, everything is taken care of by that sponsor! That surely describes **GOD**!

I thought I could work, provide for my children, and serve at the church every time the doors opened - and I did. However, my son suffered. Not having a father in the home and with me being too busy trying to keep the church going, I lost sight of my most important job: my responsibility to my children. My son was soon lured into the exciting fast lane and has had to pay dearly for that distraction…not to mention the design of the system: the school to prison pipeline. (That is a whole COMPLETELY different book! I'll write more on that in the future.) My son and I have grown a lot closer. I'm excited to see how his story continues to play out. He's such a powerful, intelligent, and handsome young, Black man!

I thought I could spearhead the Purchasing Department in excellence - and I did! I thought I could sell Real Estate and become a member of the Million Dollar Club (Top Sales) - and I did! I thought I could go back to college and complete my educational goals to become a Doctor - **YES, I DID!**

W.A.T.?

GOD has given us a tremendous capability of thought!

CHAPTER TWENTY-ONE
Forgiveness... It's For YOU!

THINKING about forgiving others when you've been wronged is not forgiveness. The *THOUGHT* of forgiving them has to be executed!

Remember:

> *FORGIVENESS IS FOR YOU... NOT FOR THE OTHER PERSON.*

By forgiving them and allowing them to go free from the prison cell in which you hold them in your heart, it produces healing and restoration for **you**. As long as you rise up in anger every time you think of them or call someone to discuss how mean they were to you "back in the day", you continue to perpetuate unforgiveness. Let them go free...and *FORGIVE* them.

The easiest **AND** hardest way to forgive others is by praying for them. Pray for them to prosper and succeed. Yes, I said pray **FOR** them. In your prayer time, instead of saying, "*Lord, they did me wrong!*", as hard as it may be, say, "*Lord, help me to forgive them. Lord, bless their new relationship. Lord, I forgive them for stealing from or gossiping about me or for talking about my mama!*" Once you pray for them, you will find it easier and easier to think good thoughts about them.

Who'd A Thought Deliverance Would Come?

Now, I'm not saying ignore the fact they cheated and gave you a sexually-transmitted disease. I'm not saying ignore the fact they refuse to pay child support while spending lavishly on another person. I'm not saying ignore the fact you were physically beaten or pistol-whipped. **NO!** I'm not saying ignore those things, for they may require further attention; however, I **AM** saying in your time of prayer, ask God to help you *FORGIVE*.

God casts our sins as far as the East is from the West, forgiving us and forgetting our wrongdoings. So, ask Him to help you forgive - then go a step further and ask God to give you supernatural amnesia regarding the wrong imposed upon you or your loved-one. God is **SO** amazing! All that He does is designed to help us live successful, prosperous, happy, and productive lives. In turn, giving Him praise and thanksgiving for all He has done and continues to do will help with the healing.

I can't help but reflect back often on my mother's brain cancer and its connection to unforgiveness. I don't believe at any time while she was still in a coherent state that she forgave my father for whatever wrong he had done. I do believe that in her mind, there was something tormenting her. That "thing" ate away at her mind (brain), ultimately generating talons of cancer all throughout her brain. Oftentimes, research directly relates physical illnesses to spiritual and mental challenges. I am left to wonder: *Did my mother's unforgiveness and unwillingness to forgive my father create the cancer that aided in her demise? Would she be here today had she received God's healing for her brain and simply forgave?*

Forgiveness... It's For YOU!

It was extremely painful separating from my mother as she left this physical world for her eternal home. I will see her again; however, the departure was excruciating because I truly believed God would heal her. I later realized: We play a part in our own healing.

W.A.T.?

You see, healthy people have no need for a doctor (see Luke 5:31). However, when you're being influenced to do things that are contrary to the original design, you need a Great Physician! You *NEED* God!

There is life after death. You have the opportunity to choose **NOW** where you will spend eternity. God loves you just that much that He will allow you to **CHOOSE** where you want to be forever!

I ask you *NOW*: **Choose Christ!**

It's so simple. All you have to do is say, "*God, forgive me for my sins. I believe you died for me, so come into my life and save me!*" If you prayed that simple prayer with all sincerity, **YOU'RE SAVED!**

Now that your spirit (which is the real you) is sealed until the day Christ returns, the process is necessary for you to get the physical and soul part of you renewed to who you - the spirit person - truly is! That's why you should read your Bible, go to church, and fellowship with like-minded believers. Remember: There is **NO** perfect church because people make up churches...and there are **NO** perfect people.

Who'd A Thought Deliverance Would Come?

I have only one biological son. I love that young man. Prior to having any children, I believed I would get married one day and give birth to a handsome, chocolate, fine male child. I did; however, my *first* born was a female. She's such a sweetheart. Still, there's something about a man-child that moved my heart to pray and ask time and again for a son. He was my riding buddy and Best Friend Forever (BFF) until his youngest sister came along. Because of the eight and 10 years apart that each child is from the other, they were **ALL** my BFFs for a long period of time.

My son had problems with being abusive towards young ladies - something he inherited from his biological father. His father would beat me for looking at a man. I'm not talking about admiring the man or even knowing anything about him...just LOOKING. (That man had some **serious** insecurity issues.) I would tell my son all the time, "*Make* **GOD** *your Father, and you'll inherit His traits. However, as long as you keep God out of the mix, you will inherit your biological father's DNA and attributes.*"

My son would also abuse the girls he would date and treat them harshly - then he would buy them expensive gifts. He would come to my home in the late evenings while I was hard at work on my Master's degree, and I would let him in to listen to his sob stories. I would watch him cry and hear him say how sorry he was to treat them that way because he really loved them, but he couldn't help himself. Of course, I would lecture and minister to him, giving him Godly wisdom and psychological directives. I could see he did not want to be an abuser, but it was easy to see the forces of darkness having their chains tightly-gripped around his life.

When you **CHOOSE** to not adopt the ways of God, guess whose ways you take on as yours? Think about it. There's no middle ground...

Forgiveness... It's For YOU!

I would get calls at 3:00 a.m. from a young lady on the other end telling me my son was hitting her and threatening to kill her. I would get angry because my sleep was interrupted. I had usually just climbed into bed (due to academia), and after that type of call I would think, **"Why doesn't she leave him like I left his father?"** I would then spend a portion of the early hours of the morning counseling and praying.

That type of call came time after time...after time!

Then, my son started calling saying his girlfriend was attacking and hurting him! Remember, now: I prayed for my son! I wanted a son **so** badly. Now, he's in his 20s and this girl is attacking him. She has already "keyed" the car (taken her keys and marked up his car) - the car I had purchased for him. Now she's getting physical with him? **OH, HECK TO THE NAW!**

I jumped into my car, and a trip that normally took 20 minutes turned into roughly seven! I left my youngest home alone to run and take care of my son! How ignorant was **that**? When I arrived, there was commotion. I told his girlfriend, *"Get out of my son's home and stay away from my family...or I am going to beat you up!"*

NOTE: I did not gather any facts. All I knew was my son was saying his life was being threatened - and I was ready to *fight*!

Needless to say, my son was big enough to take care of himself. I had no right attempting to intervene in his domestic issues. However, I did.

I know Jesus. I am a mature woman of God! I serve as a teacher in the Children's ministry. I go to the prisons to preach. I go to church every time the doors open, yet there I was...ready to **fight**? I was being used by the devil!

Who'd A Thought Deliverance Would Come?

W.A.T.?

As time passed, I grew to be really upset with myself for being influenced by the devil and allowing him to use me in such a foul fashion. I asked God to forgive me, and I know He did. I forgave myself for being so stupid and stooping so low. My heart knew I had to ask the person I directed the negative behavior towards to forgive me as well…

She and I began to talk on the phone again. I would avoid bringing up the topic. Somehow, our paths crossed and we had a "surface" conversation. The thought came again, and I did not push it down. I said to her, *"You recall when I ran to my son's rescue? I want to ask that you forgive me."* She replied, *"That's okay."*

NO! That wasn't good enough. I wanted her to know I was truly apologetic for my behavior. I wanted her to know I am a genuine Christian, and sometimes, we don't always act like we should. We must take the high road and allow Christ to be seen in us - even when we fail. I wanted her to know I would not keep pretending like nothing wrong happened. I wanted her to know why I acted in the manner I did. I needed her forgiveness, and I asked for it. I'm positive in my heart she did.

WHEN IT IS IN YOUR POWER TO CORRECT A WRONG, DO IT!

Forgiveness... It's For YOU!

There was another incident involving my son when I (again) acted ignorant. He had gotten into trouble, and his attorney was a mighty man of faith who used to sit behind my younger daughter and I every Saturday at prayer in our church.

(My church holds corporate prayer on Saturdays for those who wish to come and pray corporately - as the Bible instructs. We have prayer on Sunday before church begins as well; however, Saturday prayer is more relaxed. It is **ALL** prayer for a full hour.)

Well, the attorney and I would chat. He and my daughter would discuss universities. He was maybe a few years older than my son - a young professional. He represented my son in a legal matter, and I didn't feel he was putting much effort into the case. I felt the representation was inadequate, so I terminated his services. *(He made me aware I couldn't terminate him because I never retained his services...my son's friend did.)*

Anyway, we would pass each other regularly every Sunday and would look in the other direction whenever we would come into close proximity of each other. We were both mature Christians (or so we claimed) and we weren't even speaking to one another - **IN THE LORD'S HOUSE!** Although I did not like his level of work regarding my son's case, we were brother- and sister-in-Christ. Just as we do not like seeing our children on bad terms with each other, I think God was disappointed with us being on non-speaking terms.

Mind you, it was a long-time desire of mine to meet a 100-year-old man who was still very active in ministry. He was the one who coined the phrase, **"Think about it."** The attorney made that meeting possible. I had no right to get disgruntled to the point that I stopped speaking to that attorney! I was so grateful for his act of kindness, then later, so *MAD* I wouldn't even speak? Who'd a thought I would act like that?

Who'd A Thought Deliverance Would Come?

Again, I mustered up the courage and communicated to him that we profess Christ. We should not be ignoring each other and pretending like we don't see each other. I asked him to forgive me. Just because I was disappointed with his services, that gave me no right to treat him as a non-person - and vice-versa. Who gives me the right? That same ill will can rebound because what a man sows, he reaps.

Treat people like you want to be treated! That's the bottom line!

I am so thankful I asked the attorney to forgive me for my evil-influenced behavior of pressing my lips together tightly whenever I saw him. No, we were not cussing each other out. No, we were not stealing each other's wealth. No, we were not committing adultery. No, we were not shooting guns at each other. We were operating in unforgiveness - and that is just as deadly as any other sin! The attorney has since departed this Earth, and having made my wrongs right with him affords me peace.

Forgiveness is a powerful tool. Learn to execute it. The wages (payment) for sin is still death (see Romans 6:23). Ask my mother! **UNFORGIVENESS IS DEADLY!**

God **commands** us to *LOVE ONE ANOTHER!* When you're working honestly for your family on the job and that fine man gives you too much positive, flirtatious attention and you know he's married *BUT* your husband or boyfriend left you with the kids for another woman and you haven't had any "male attention" in a long time, cut it **OFF** before it starts! Don't be a *HOMEWRECKER!* Indiscretions will affect his wife, your children, him, **AND** definitely you (and I don't mean in a positive way). There are always repercussions for negative actions…

> *THE HARVEST IS ALWAYS GREATER THAN THE SEED YOU SOW. WHAT YOU SOW, YOU WILL DEFINITELY REAP... BUT IN A GREATER MEASURE.*

When you're blessed with a good man and he's tempted by some cutie pie, you do **NOT** want to have sown seeds of infidelity, adultery, and disharmony. Just tell Mr. Fine that he *IS* fine. Stroke his ego, but tell him he's not fine enough for you to fall short of who you know you are. That way, you won't need to expect deliverance to come because you will nip that silliness in the bud! Starve that fleshly desire, and it will die! I promise you.

CHAPTER TWENTY-TWO
How Does Deliverance Come?

I've been forgiven for much; thus, I am capable of loving much. My heart is right. I'm able to rationalize why others do what they do because I was once where they are. As opposed to judging, I can relate.

I hear folks say, "*I would never do anything like that*", and I think to myself, "*Apparently, you've never done* **ANYTHING** *wrong or the devil has decided to totally bypass you and never try to yoke you up with any of his foolish, addictive behaviors. You might want to check your* **PRIDE***!*"

The enemy may have never yoked you up with drugs, pornography, or sex sins, but he's **DEFINITELY** been on his job working on your thoughts. Just the *THOUGHT* of you thinking you're better than someone else is an open door for self-deception - and that's **HORRIFIC**!

"But I say unto you, that whosoever looketh on a woman to lust after her hath committed adultery with her already in his heart."
(Matthew 5:28)

"Stinking Thinking" requires some deliverance!

You see, deliverance is for all of us. We're ever-evolving and being transformed into someone better *(hopefully)* than we were yesterday. The Madman of Gadarenes was cutting himself in the graveyard with stones. Many people today are cutting themselves in the corporate setting with embezzlement and are in need of deliverance. They can't stop…it's an addiction! They get away with it once and get 'hooked', taking more and more and more.

How Does Deliverance Come?

We've seen it happen with corporate giants and banks in our day. Those individuals needed deliverance from the addictive monkey of greed that was riding on their backs. They got on that merry-go-round and couldn't find the **'STOP'** button. Still others are addicted to power.

One of my favorite reads is *Good to Great* by Jim Collins. In his book, he talks about the Nucor System of getting from just being good to actually becoming exceptional. Many times, in business, the term is used regarding people being your most important asset because people are who actually make the business wheel turn. However, Jim Collins highlights *exemplary* productivity. It is derived from not just 'people being your most important asset, but the **RIGHT** people'. It doesn't matter if they have a Doctorate, but rather *character* is what's needed to be exceptional.

People who will steal from the company or won't come back to work on time after lunch because they are somewhere getting high are not the people you are looking for. You want people who are delivered from those success-blockers.

The information in this book of deliverance will help those wrong people become the **RIGHT** people by getting delivered and staying delivered so they can be a business-builder - be it their own business **OR** yours!

CHAPTER TWENTY-THREE
How to STAY in the Deliverance-Zone

The key to staying delivered is ongoing starvation of those things that brought about the addiction (whatever it may be) in the first place, reprogramming your mind with the Word of God, and other supplemental books, movies, plays, and fun activities. Staying in the Deliverance-Zone is a nonstop process! We never stop learning, growing, and changing. We never want to go back to what we were...that 'thing' that held us captive, doing something we did not truly desire to do.

I've had temporary deliverance before, but **PERMANENT** is so much better! See, I thought I had it all under control once I stopped running behind that daily "get high". The problem was I didn't reprogram my *MIND* with a replacement. So, there I went again...back to the mud...to the vomit!

See, you may not be addicted to drugs, porno, cigarettes, or marijuana. You may not be guilty of company fraud, cheating on your spouse or even your taxes. There is a great deal of folks who are, and knowing how to give them insight on how to be free is extremely beneficial. Throwing a lifeline and infusing people with the life support of Jesus' love and saving grace is vital in the times in which we now live - especially **RIGHT NOW** with the opiate crisis in the United States being an epidemic.

Drug addictions usually don't travel alone. They typically bring with them thievery, fraud, embezzlement, unearthed sexual preferences, adultery, unhealthy lifestyle choices, and so much more. They are evil spirits that are using the person to carry out *their* orders.

How to STAY in the Deliverance-Zone

Have you ever wondered why people act differently when they drink "spirits" (liquor)? **THINK!**

I've been thinking of strategies for Triage Units to be opened around the country, constructing multiple units located near drug-infested areas where people can come in on a daily basis and get infused with the Word of God. Perhaps have a Triage Unit near each church and put those who desire healing on life support - a steady diet of the Word of God and maybe a sandwich bag daily after sitting for 30 minutes of said infusion. A daily dose of the Word of God can change a life forever! I haven't worked out all the logistics yet, but I do know what worked for me. I'd be willing to bet it will work for others. If we sit idly by and do nothing, the epidemic will continue to spread and, just like cancer, you want to treat it before it becomes deadly.

Of course, there are people who minister to drug addicts on the streets and give them food; however, I am unaware of any organizations that are doing it on a daily basis with the stipulation of gaining concept of why it is important to nourish their spirit and renew their minds to get from that place where they are.

Deliverance comes in multiple forms, but it does come!

Just as some women have children by way of adoption, others have delivery via a C-section (cesarean), others choose natural birth, and still others prefer receiving an epidural. Some have enjoyed deliverance supernaturally, others instantaneously, while others have received with medical assistance. Others have experienced a series of events.

If you **WANT** it, it's available for you. Deliverance comes!

Who'd A Thought Deliverance Would Come?

In Mark Chapter 5, the Madman got his deliverance by encountering Jesus and having the controlling demons cast out. The woman with the issue of blood had to take a risk and fight her way through the crowd to touch Jesus' garment to get what she came for. Jairus had to hold fast to his belief that deliverance for his child would come to fruition.

THEY ALL RECEIVED WHAT THEY NEEDED FROM JESUS!

Somehow, I went from a studious, destined for great success, beautiful young lady to one who gave new meaning to the word *BAD*! My parents were so busy working, they did not concern themselves with teaching me about adulthood, staying focused, and not allowing any wicked thing to come before me.

SIDENOTE: During my last conversation with my father, I asked if there was anything he could have done differently in life, what would it have been? His response was he wished he had spent more time supporting me in all of my endeavors...

CHAPTER TWENTY-FOUR
It's Time to SILENCE Those Negative Voices

"While you're changing and experiencing supernatural metamorphosis into that beautiful, new creation, always give God thanks and remember: A butterfly will NEVER fly...thinking like a caterpillar."
~ George W. Byfield ~

There is **POWER** in thanksgiving. Start a 'Thankful Journal'. Jot down five things nightly that you've experienced that day that you're thankful for. Each time you're blessed to be favored in some way or given an innovative thought to save your company millions or do your work in a smarter not harder way, say, "*Thank you, Lord!*" or "*That's the favor of God!*" Thanksgiving perpetuates more blessings to be thankful for!

You work on that 'going nowhere' job. You're in that 'not for you' relationship and want out. You're overweight, but don't want to stop eating. Your kids are on the path to destruction and won't listen to reason. You're in a court battle, and no one will call a truce. You're never included. You're addicted to shopping. You're being talked about wrongly. You're being 'wretched' to the point you don't even like yourself. Will things ever change? Will things ever get better?

Listen to me and listen **CLOSELY:** *DELIVERANCE HAS ALREADY COME!* Deliverance is in you! The Deliverer is in you! He's already opened the door and set you free from all that foolishness and those strongholds! Whenever you're ready to be free, just walk through the door! What you want is already in you! Manifest your deliverance!

Who'd A Thought Deliverance Would Come?

The Holy Spirit is a gentleman. He's not going to force-feed you and **MAKE** you take what has already been afforded. The door to your freedom is open! You're free **RIGHT NOW!**

Profoundly stated by Terri Savelle Foy, *"You can only conquer your past when you focus on your future."*

See through the windshield and not the rearview mirror. The only time I choose to look back is when I'm desirous of relating to and elevating someone else up to where I am. I can truly say, *"I was once where you are"*. Otherwise, I don't allow my mind to drift back into that hell. Where your mind and thoughts go, you have a tendency to move in that direction...

When I'm shopping and hear an old song from the 60s, my mind immediately takes me to where and who I was with when that tune was hot. Most of the time, I'll jerk the slack out of my mind and say, *"Alright, Lucy: Come on out of there!"* See, my spirit - the real me - has to let the body know who's boss because my body and mind can really steer me toward some places I should not go. (During my years of studying Psychology, one course that was quite intriguing was 'The Mind'. The book referenced how the mind is **not** the brain.)

I smoked cigarettes from the time I was a junior in high school and, from that juncture, to 20+ years. I didn't have Nicoderm, the nicotine patch, nor smokeless cigarettes. I had **DELIVERANCE**! I built myself up with prayer and relying on the Greater One in me. One day, I made up my mind that I was going to draw the line in the sand, and that was my 'walking on water day'. You see, I **HAD** to step out of the boat.

Deliverance was already with me, but fear, torment, voices of others, and the enemy told me I couldn't be delivered. I'm here to tell you: **YOU** can be delivered and (better than that), *YOU'RE ALREADY DELIVERED!*

It's Time to SILENCE Those Negative Voices

My drugs of choice were heroin and cocaine…daily. Yours may be TV, out-of-control shopping, cigarettes, an uncontrollable sex addiction, sick and sinful thoughts, backstabbing, lying, child predator, deceit, stripping, multiple sex partners, and/or wild partying. How about this one: overeating! **STARVE IT ALL…***CONTINUOUSLY! GO FREE!*

Once you make up your mind, it's a done deal! **AMAZING GRACE** shows up on the scene!

Thomas Jefferson is quoted as saying, "*If you want something you have never had, you must be willing to do something you have never done*". One way to accomplish that is to apply Steven Covey's *7 Habits of Highly Effective People*, one of which is 'beginning with the end in mind'! Think about where you want to go in life, what you want to become, and what legacy you want to leave behind. Get a picture of that on the inside of you. "See" where you want to wind up at the end of your life and focus on it. Develop that picture on the inside by spending 5, 10, 15, 20, to 30 minutes a day meditating on it in a quiet, uninterrupted space. Watch that new picture enlarge. Albert Einstein is quoted as saying, "*Imagination is everything. It is the preview of life's coming attractions.*"

When you go to the movies, you always see coming attractions of upcoming movie releases. Well, watch your own upcoming realities on the screen of your mind by using your God-given imagination for healthy, wealthy, successful, and prosperous movies of your future!

Step out on faith! You'll be astonished! You will say, **"Self, I didn't know I could do that! Go on with your GOOD self, Self! You're all that, Self!"** (There's nothing wrong with self-talk.) Then, begin to thank and praise God because it's **HIS** power that always causes you to triumph! You ain't nothing but a *WINNER!*

Who'd A Thought Deliverance Would Come?

Don't tell me you can't stop eating. I've been so fat, I couldn't see my toes! I thought I could never stop eating sugar, and I've done better than that: I've gone for 21 days with only water, green vegetable juices, and herb teas...and you can, too! Once you come to the realization of how powerful you are, you will take on the spirit of overeating and stop making excuses regarding why you're overweight. Ask God for help. He loves to get involved in every area of our lives. **SPEAK** to your metabolism and tell it to speed up!

I'm becoming all I'm destined to be with the hope of releasing you to become great and fulfill your purpose.

> *"Our deepest fear is not that we are inadequate. Our deepest fear is that we are powerful beyond measure. It is our light, not our darkness, that most frightens us. We ask ourselves, "Who am I to be brilliant, gorgeous, talented, fabulous?" Actually, who are you not to be? You are a child of God. Your playing small does not serve the world. There is nothing enlightened about shrinking so that other people won't feel insecure around you. We are all meant to shine, as children do. We were born to make manifest the glory of God that is within us. It is not just in some of us; it is in everyone. And as we let our own light shine, we unconsciously give other people permission to do the same. As we are liberated from our own fear, our presence automatically liberates others."*
> ~ Marianne Williamson from *A Return to Love: Reflections on the Principles of a Course in Miracles*

See, I was **SO** jacked up! God has made me new. I decided I was displeased with the life I was living - living in Lodebar (see 2 Samuel 9)...down below the bar!

I had to make the decision to change. I had to decide I wanted to experience **DELIVERANCE**. Once I made up my mind and **SAID IT,** *IT CAME TO FRUITION!*

It's Time to SILENCE Those Negative Voices

YOU HAVE TO DECREE IT in order for it to be *ESTABLISHED* (see Job 22:28). You can't sit around moping and hoping for it to come...

> *"For by thy words, thou shalt be justified, and by thy words, thou shalt be condemned."*
> *(Matthew 12:37)*

JUSTIFY YOURSELF...don't *CONDEMN* yourself! Don't order a negative self-fulfilling prophesy. Order **LIFE** and *LIFE* more abundantly!

In a nutshell, **SPEAK DELIVERANCE!**

Jesse Duplantis says, "*Admit it, quit it, and forget it!*" I say, **"Acknowledge it, starve it, and end it!"** Grab hold of the new you and cultivate a person who you always dreamed you could become. Believe me: You are the deciding witness. Once I decided I didn't want to smoke anymore, I drew the line in the sand and decreed, "I'm done with smoking." I quit - after 20 years of feeding the habit. You see, no one gave me a shot. I didn't take a pill, wear a patch, or receive any other form of exterior assistance to quit. Deliverance was there...inside of me...**ALL THE TIME!** I decided I wanted to quit doing drugs. I decided I wanted to quit smoking. I decided I wanted to live a life of purity. I **DECIDED** - and *DELIVERANCE* was there.

At any time you decide, deliverance will be there for you as well.

Who'd A Thought Deliverance Would Come?

The art of deliverance is very similar to the eagle's way of assisting its eaglets with flight. They take the initial nudging to get out there and soar, and they give it their best; however, if they are incapable of handling it initially, they come back into the comfort of the nest. When confidence is nurtured. They're given that nudge to jump, defeat the fear, and begin to soar!

God is nudging us continually to get out there and at least *ATTEMPT* to soar. He will be the wind beneath our wings!

CHAPTER TWENTY-FIVE
Prompting of the Spirit

For a **VERY** long time, I desired quitting the enumerable strongholds that held me in bondage; however, I needed a little nudging. Some refer to it as 'Prompting of the Spirit'. I needed the confident assurance that I could actually do it. Initially, it was a bit frightening leaping over into the unknown world of freedom. I had heard horror stories of how painful withdrawal from drugs were and how one would have dry heaves, runny nose, coughing, and chills - symptoms (supposedly) of the monkey not giving up the free ride on one's back. I liken that 'experience' to the boy who was delivered from a demon that threw him into a fire (see Matthew 17:15-18). That demon didn't want to let go. It needed a body to act out through.

Emotional trauma is sometimes associated with letting go of behaviors, habits, people, and addictions that have been a part of your life for long periods of time. You get to choose! Is the trauma and drama necessary? Must you give way to your feelings? Some of us are stronger than others, so you will have to be the judge of that. Some have higher tolerance levels for pain than others. We're all different. I'm here to give you support from **my** experience.

Let me tell you about *MY* experience.

I had **NONE** of the withdrawal symptoms during my deliverance from drug addiction. I experienced **NO** withdrawal symptoms during my deliverance from nicotine and cigarette smoking. I experienced **NO** withdrawal symptoms from any form of sex outside of marriage that I previously engaged in.

JESUS SET ME FREE, AND I AM FREE, INDEED!

Who'd A Thought Deliverance Would Come?

Now, *HERE'S* the kicker: I have been free for over 30 years, and the suggestive thoughts from the enemy that try to plague my thoughts are where the battle has to be a 'fight to the finish'! Thus, I continue to fill my mind with God's powerful Word and am always able to annul, quench, annihilate, and take down the thoughts that are contrary to my being a **WINNER** in every battle.

Joyce Meyer wrote a book entitled *Battlefield of the Mind* that resonates with me. On page 169, she writes, "*Nothing is closer to us than our own thoughts. Therefore, if we will fill our mind with the Lord, it will bring Him into our consciousness and we will begin to enjoy a fellowship with Him that will bring joy, peace, and victory to our everyday life...Think about what you are thinking about.*"

I walk around thinking great thoughts - thoughts of grandeur and thoughts of deliverance. I sing to myself and the Lord. I smile in my heart and keep one plastered on my face for this reason: **I AM HAPPY AND FREE!** Those thoughts and singing are a result of many years of sowing Bible verses, sitting under anointed teachings week after week, reading Christian books, and delving into books that promote positive thinking. I went to church...a *LOT*. I attend World Changers Church International and hear Pastor Dollar preach day in and day out - every Sunday, every Wednesday, and prayer on Saturdays. I went so much, my friends teased me about being at church every time the doors opened - **BUT** they didn't know how much bad thinking I needed to have uprooted and how desperately I needed to have new thoughts implanted. I was working on building a new foundation.

Creflo Dollar taught me the Word of God with simplicity. I became stronger and stronger. I relished in the fact that I was being teased! I have **JOY** that has come as a result of being at the church...every time the doors were opened!

Prompting of the Spirit

"Do not be conformed to this world (this age), [fashioned after and adapted to its external, superficial customs], but be transformed (changed) by the [entire] renewal of your mind [by its new ideas and its new attitude], so that you may prove [for yourselves] what is the good and acceptable and perfect will of God, even the thing which is good and acceptable and perfect [in His sight for you]."
(Romans 12:2)

That is what we do once we are born again and delivered from bondages... Renew our minds!

For many years, I only read the Bible and only listened to Christian music. However, now that I am anchored in my "new creature" lifestyle, I enjoy listening to *SOME* music that is not necessarily labeled as "Christian" music; however, I make certain the non-Christian music is of a positive nature and cannot diminish, delete, or replace years of planting great seed in my new soil.

I am an avid reader, enjoying books by cutting-edge strategists, business moguls, motivational authors, and spiritual greats. When my new husband comes on the scene, we'll enjoy the sexy sounds of Anita Baker, smooth grooves by KEM, and other favorite sensuous artists that 'take you there'. Obviously, I cannot listen to them sing on a regular basis and not become sexually aroused. Boundaries... We must set boundaries for ourselves!

Who'd A Thought Deliverance Would Come?

Remember: It all starts with a thought, and thoughts can trigger negative **OR** positive behaviors. **THINK** about what you're thinking about! Don't allow people or negative thoughts to rent space in your mind. *EVICT THEM!*

> *DON'T LET NEGATIVE AND TOXIC PEOPLE RENT SPACE IN YOUR HEAD. RAISE THE RENT AND KICK THEM OUT!*
> *~ ROBERT TEW ~*

CHAPTER TWENTY-SIX
Quiet Time: Time to Meditate

Your "stinking thinking" must be extracted and replaced with thoughts that are in line with Philippians 4:8:

"For the rest, brethren, whatever is true, whatever is worthy of reverence and is honorable and seemly, whatever is just, whatever is pure, whatever is lovely and lovable, whatever is kind and winsome and gracious, if there is any virtue and excellence, if there is anything worthy of praise, think on and weigh and take account of these things [fix your minds on them]."

Remember: You are what you think about. Think wealthy, successful, overcoming thoughts - then you have the potential to become those things! The thoughts don't appear in your thinking by mere osmosis; they must be fed to your brain, soul, and spirit consistently. Afterwards, you must incorporate a time of turning those thoughts into confessions!

Every book I've read while studying habits of successful men and women share how they all rise early and take time to quiet themselves...and meditate *(another word for envisioning, imagining, and seeing inside what you want to see outside)*.

Corporations teach their staff and sales forces how to interject positive confessions into their work and train them on how to believe they will get that sale or win that contract. Thinking and speaking the truth is the only way to go!

Who'd A Thought Deliverance Would Come?

God told Abraham he would be the father of many nations, so much so that Abraham's descendants would exceed the number of the stars and the sand on the sea. Abraham would go out and look at the stars and the sand on the sea to remind himself of the promise of what was to come. Create a vision board of what you desire to see come to fruition in your life. Never ever give up! God waited until Abraham and Sarah were well past the age of giving birth in order to defy all odds (see Genesis 17, Genesis 18, and Genesis 22:17). If it looks like deliverance is delayed, **HOLD ON!** *IT'S COMING!*

If you are unable to go out and look at what reminds you of your promises (like Abraham did), use your imagination. If you can't purchase books or paintings, use your imagination. If you can envision it, it still has the potential to manifest. Even if you **CAN** purchase books and items that will help you envision your dreams coming to reality, *STILL USE YOUR IMAGINATION!*

> *"Imagination is everything. It is the preview of life's coming attractions."*
> ~ Albert Einstein ~

See yourself free from that addiction that's trying to hold you captive. Find a picture of yourself **BEFORE** the addiction took hold of you - or get a picture of someone you admire. Look at that picture and think about it! *IMAGINE* being that picture.

Jacob desired deliverance from his trickery father-in-law. If he can carve stripes in wood above a watering hole for flocks to look at before they drank water, and by looking at those stripes, the flocks produced striped cattle, don't tell me you can't look at a picture or imagine your new life and not see it come to pass (see Genesis 30:36-43).

Quiet Time: Time to Meditate

Surround yourself with what you desire to blossom into. If you would like to attain well-read status, purchase books - not apparel. Forego another pair of shoes and buy some books.

My youngest daughter says I equate *everything* to shoes. While studying in London, she suffered a tremendous loss. I said, "*We could have purchased five pairs of Christian Louboutins with that money!*" However, we did remind the thief that he would have to return sevenfold of what he stole.

If your calling is in the Arts, acquire paintings or prints that will give a visual to remind you of the artist you have trapped inside. If dancing is your thing, carve out 30 minutes three times a week to choreograph that award-winning performance.

Life is for the living, and you, my friend, are a **FAITH FORCE** with tremendous ability to *FAITH FOCUS!*

You were created for a purpose. Deep inside of you is the desire to do and become what you were predestined to accomplish here on Earth. It is challenging to fulfill your destiny with uncontrollable baggage, so get set free!

> *THE GRAVEYARD IS THE RICHEST PLACE ON EARTH.*

Who'd A Thought Deliverance Would Come?

Les Brown is quoted as saying, "*The graveyard is the richest place on Earth because it is here that you will find all the hopes and dreams that were never fulfilled, the books that were never written, the songs that were never sung, the inventions that were never shared, and the cures that were never discovered - all because someone was too afraid to take that first step, keep with the problem, or not determined to carry out their dream.*"

The **world** is waiting on you to get rid of that unnecessary baggage and go free. The **world** is waiting on you to be who God created you to be from the foundation of the world. People are in need of your song, your book, that movie that compels people to soar, that composed piece that gives Beethoven a wakeup call, that innovative invention that makes life easier for someone to live, that exhilarating dance that warrants a standing ovation, and so on!

COME ON! RECEIVE YOUR DELIVERANCE TODAY! SOMEONE IS WAITING ON YOU! THE WORLD IS WAITING FOR YOU TO MANIFEST!

You have something great to offer. Don't keep folks waiting!

Oh. And don't tell me 'your time has passed'. Colonel Sanders didn't start Kentucky Fried Chicken until he was 65 years old!

Rewrite your own story, my friend!

CHAPTER TWENTY-SEVEN
The Harvest is ALWAYS Greater Than the Seed!

Practice mindfulness. Think about what you're thinking about. If it's not bringing you success, **STOP** thinking about it. Discontinue discussing others in a negative light.

What you sow, you definitely reap. The harvest is **ALWAYS** greater than the seed - and that applies to both positive and negative aspects of life.

Let me share something with you that may be a little deep. *REALIZE THIS:* You're already where you're pressing to get to. Relax. Rest. Breathe. Get in God's flow and allow it to happen.

I tried to get free from drugs by going to rehab, staying inside the house, and getting high "only on the weekend". None of that gave me lasting results. **ALL I had to do was get in God's flow and rest!** I didn't have to struggle to get free from cigarettes. I never had withdrawal symptoms when I allowed God to deliver me.

Remember to use your imagination. Oral Roberts subtitled his book *Still Doing the Impossible* with "When You See the Invisible, You Can Do the Impossible". In his book, he said, "*I was seeing the invisible; therefore, doing the impossible was just around the corner.*"

WHEN YOU SEE THE INVISIBLE, YOU CAN DO THE IMPOSSIBLE.

Who'd A Thought Deliverance Would Come?

Okay. You have been given ideas to encourage and strengthen you in taking the deliverance that is yours. Do not settle for less! Do not fear!

If you have children out there on drugs or engaging in criminal or non-Godly behavior, stay vigilant. Fight for them in prayer. Stay the course. Deliverance is available for them.

It looked like Mary had been having sex outside of marriage before giving birth to Jesus Christ. It may **look like** there is no hope for your unsaved loved-one, estranged relative, co-worker, or friend. I'm here to tell you there is not only hope, but there's complete deliverance!

One thing to keep in mind: The fight is fixed - and, according to the Book of Revelation - **WE WIN!** If you can stay focused on the promises of God, keeping your mind affixed to the truth and not what *appears* to be real, you'll see the situation change.

For me, it took well over 20 years of relatives praying for me, but they stayed the course, remained vigilant, and were ever awake and alert. They believed God for my **total** deliverance - and they saw the end of their faith!

A SATANIC INFLUENCE IS ALMOST ALWAYS BEHIND THE STAGNATIONS, FAILURES, AND LOSSES THAT PEOPLE EXPERIENCE IN LIFE.

The Harvest is ALWAYS Greater Than the Seed!

Bishop David O. Oyedepo states in his book, *Commanding the Supernatural*:

"A satanic influence is almost always behind the stagnations, failures, and losses that people experience in life. The sad thing is this: Because of ignorance and insensitivity, many Christians become vulnerable to the wickedness of the devil. Many are diligent, but only a few are vigilant. Many are sincere, but only a few are sensitive. Don't be deceived. If Satan tempted Christ - the Son of God - he will attempt to control anyone else. The truth is that every accomplishment of destiny attracts the devil's attention. He will do everything to frustrate it."

With your newfound freedom - your **DELIVERANCE** - some people (including the devil) are not going to be happy for you. They will try to lure you back into the old way of living, coping with life while being in bondage…BUT you are no longer ignorant of Satan's devices. You know as you renew your mind, you can withstand not only the devil, but anyone else who would not celebrate **DELIVERANCE** with you.

Who'd A Thought Deliverance Would Come?

CONCLUSION

In Mark Chapter 5, the Madman got set free from cutting himself in the tombs - the dead places of life. I've related myself to that man and have shared a stunning and transparent parallel of my life with similar battles.

Additionally, in the same chapter, the woman with the issue of blood was set free after having been constantly bleeding…**FOR TWELVE YEARS.** Can you imagine that? That woman tried everything (just as I did) to get set free.

Although Jairus (the man with the ill 12-year-old daughter in Mark Chapter 5) had requested Jesus' help prior to the woman with the issue of blood interrupting his request, he didn't lose heart. Time appeared wasted to get the help he so desired for his daughter, but he continued believing Jesus was the answer he sought.

I was addicted to drugs and tried 'everything' to get set free: drug treatment programs, methadone clinics, will-power, empty positive confessions, and more - but **ONLY GOD** brought about a permanent change…a permanent freedom…a permanent deliverance…*A PERMANENT JOY!*

Many times, during our wait for deliverance, it appears to ourselves and our loved-ones that others are getting their help and we are 'forgotten' by God…

Others' children are saved and off of drugs.

Others receive their new homes.

Others obtain new careers and job promotions.

Others get brand new cars and are debt-free.

Conclusion

Others' businesses are prospering beyond measure.

Others get a new husband, wife, and/or long-awaited child.

Jairus stayed in faith, even after a messenger told him it was too late for his daughter to receive help. She had died while Jesus was on the way to her. Jesus reassured Jairus that he was to **ONLY BELIEVE.** That is what I'm assuring *YOU* on today: **BELIEVE! DELIVERANCE COMES!** Sometimes, it shows up subtly. Other times, it's over the *TOP!* If you **BELIEVE**, you will see the goodness of the Lord in the land of the living.

Don't faint! Don't quit! **NEVER STOP BELIEVING!**

Remember: Jesus is **THE RESURRECTION!** Selah. Take a moment to pause right now and calmly think on that. He specializes in bringing *LIFE* to dead situations. Ask Mary and Martha what He did for their brother (see John 11)! **HECK...ASK ME!**

Sometimes, it appears our deliverance is not coming, but I ask you, beg of you, appeal to you, **PLEAD** with you: Don't get off the mark! Stay in faith! *ONLY BELIEVE YOUR DELIVERANCE IS DEFINITELY GOING TO MANIFEST!*

To tell you the truth, it's really contingent upon when you're ready for it. Jairus received what He asked of Jesus. His daughter was raised back to life, only after all internal negative dialogue was shut *DOWN* and all external negative dialogue was *silenced*. Jesus had to put the folks out of the man's house because they were not on the same page as He was. Sometimes, we have to keep our mouths closed as we shut down our thoughts that go against what we know to be **TRUTH!**

Who'd A Thought Deliverance Would Come?

DID YOU KNOW? The number 12 is very significant in Mark Chapter 5. The woman with the issue of blood had bled for 12 years (Mark 5:25). Jairus' daughter was 12 years of age (Mark 5:42). Twelve is considered a perfect number, symbolizing God's power and authority.

Doreen Virtue expounds further stating, *"The number 12 is a combination of the numbers '1', which means, "Stay positive", and '2', which means, "Keep the faith". Together, 12 is a strong message to stay positive, optimistic, and filled with faith...because your positive thoughts and faith will create a positive outcome."*

As you take the leap of faith and believe you can receive your deliverance, you will find it was there waiting for you all the time. The ability to *SOAR* was right there waiting for you - and guess what? You will find it easier to take on the next step up your success ladder as you continue to lay aside every weight that so easily tries to keep you down.

You see, all it takes is that first victory. From that point on, you know the methodology to achieve deliverance from **ANY** yoke that attempts to hold you back. God did it for me once in one arena called 'drug addiction'. He did it for me again in other arenas: alcohol and cigarettes. He did it for me a third time in a different field of soaring in business when others were failing. God has caused me to gain deliverance over every situation I wanted to be ***delivered from!*** Sometimes, it takes me a little longer to muster up the confidence to step out and grab hold of what I know is there waiting for me; however, each time I take a step, **MANIFESTATION** of deliverance from what held me captive is right there!

Conclusion

Earlier in this book, I spoke about having drawn a line in the sand regarding quitting cigarettes. Going after my deliverance can be summed up in Steve Harvey's 'Jump with Steve Letter, Action Step #11 (referencing an email I received December 11, 2016): *"The line in the sand represents your personal set of standards. These are standards that are set in black and white and represent what is acceptable and allowable in your life and what isn't. It's what you will put up with and what you won't. A lack of standards and boundaries will cause you to slip into relationships, business deals, career moves, financial situations, behaviors, and actions that take you further from your goals, impacts your self-esteem, and reduces the quality of your life."*

I was no longer willing to put up with coughing, hacking, running out of the house at all hours of the night to purchase a pack of cigarettes, breathing second-hand smoke, and having to smoke after every meal. No longer was I willing to expose my children to them breathing **MY** second-hand smoke. No longer was I willing to allow the demon spirit to use me to fulfill its desire. I valued myself and my children enough to say, **"HEY! ENOUGH IS ENOUGH!"**

I heard a preacher talking about being free, and it ignited in my spirit the power I needed. That very day, my faith had been topped with icing on the cake by the message. Although I was only a Babe-in-Christ at the time, I literally took my foot and used it to draw an imaginary line in my sister's driveway and said, **"That's it!"** Since that moment, I no longer desired to smoke cigarettes - and I don't battle with withdrawals. *HOWEVER*, I must admit…there was a significant advantage: My palate was awakened to how delicious food really is (smoking dulls the sense of taste). I enjoyed eating again and gained weight, but I recognized overeating as a new stronghold immediately.

Who'd A Thought Deliverance Would Come?

The same way I won the battles against drugs and cigarettes, I received deliverance from overeating and was able to rid myself of the excessive weight gain. I began studying healthier eating habits to replace the old, unhealthy ones. I also began practicing healthy lifestyle choices, including exercising, into my daily regimen.

Right now, I continue on this journey of life, gaining **MORE** victorious deliverances as I go.

Deliverance from people trying to make me fit in their mold and trying to keep me where they think I should be.

Deliverance from adding commentary to conversations, even if I'm knowledgeable. Scripture says, "...*don't cast your pearls before swine*" (Matthew 7:6). It is not necessary to let people know what you're thinking **all** of the time.

> *PRACTICE THE VOCABULARY OF SILENCE.*

I encourage you to receive deliverance from negative thoughts and from speaking negative words - even in jest. Words have the power to manifest. We operate in the Kingdom of God and should say what **HE** says. Receive deliverance from ignorance (not knowing) by becoming educated and reading books that further enhance your knowledge base. Receive deliverance from allowing the enemy to run rampant in areas that concern you and your family by using **ALL** authority given to you by our Heavenly Father!

Conclusion

Remember: We need to feed our spirit with new thoughts. Therefore, it is important to connect to a church that believes the Bible and teaches the Word of God unapologetically and uncompromisingly. There is no perfect church; however, there are many great churches today that will teach the Word of God and nothing else.

They have weekly impartations for you on how to operate in your new life with your new manual - **The HOLY B-I-B-L-E!** There are also 24-hour TV networks and countless apps that teach the Word of God, making it easy to live victoriously - the way you were designed to live.

CHANGE YOUR THOUGHTS BY DOWNLOADING GOD'S THOUGHTS.

Who'd A Thought Deliverance Would Come?

DELIVERANCE CONFESSIONS & AFFIRMATIONS

Following are some quick confessions you can speak out loud daily (you can also obtain a copy of my 'Deliverance Confessions' on MP3 or CD by visiting Amazon.com). Say the confessions out loud as you're getting dressed in the mornings or driving down the highway. Use your creative power by speaking God's Words in faith out of your mouth.

FAITH FOCUS

+

EXECUTION

=

FAITH FORCE!

You are **UNSTOPPABLE!** *THAT'S* who you are in Christ!

When a boxer wins a championship, he will be challenged again and again for that title. The same applies to deliverance. As I was delivered from drugs, I was challenged. I stood my ground, though. I did not fall for the 'Okey-doke' (temptation) - and I kept my deliverance! I really enjoy being **FREE**. There is **NO BONDAGE** holding me!

Let's do this!

Deliverance Confessions & Affirmations

Whatever you're desiring to be set free from, fill in the blank with the name of that 'thing'. Make your confessions and affirmations out loud. Don't "just read" them. God **hears** you…*and so does the enemy!*

- I have authority over you _____ (name the addiction). (Mark 1:27) I command you to release your hold on me! Get your sick talons out of my life **NOW**, in Jesus Christ's Name!
- I am free. Jesus has set me free. He who the Son sets free is free, indeed. I am free, indeed! (John 8:36)
- I am fearfully- and wonderfully-made. (Psalm 139:14)
- I am beautiful. I am whole. (Ecclesiastes 3:11)
- I am healthy, happy, and wealthy. (3 John 2)
- The Lord saved me by a great deliverance. (1 Chronicles 11:14) Deliverance has come! I am delivered and set free - now and forever more.
- God has given me such deliverance as this! (Ezra 9:13) I am delivered from the addictive spirit of _____.
- I am a new creature in Christ. Old things are passed away. Behold, all things are become new! (2 Corinthians 5:17). I am no longer controlled by _____. I am free and new, in Jesus' Name.
- I am free to preach deliverance to the captives, and recovering of sight to the blind, to set at liberty them that are bruised. (Luke 4:18) I was held captive by _____, but now I am free! I am a light for others to see.
- Sin has no power over me. God has set me free. He brings out those which are bound with chains. (Psalm 68:6) I am no longer bound with the chain of _____.
- My faith has made me whole; I go in peace, and I am whole from that addiction. (Mark 5:34) Thank you, Lord, for delivering me and for making me whole.

Who'd A Thought Deliverance Would Come?

- The Lord will make an utter end: affliction shall not rise up the second time. (Nahum 1:9) Thank you, Lord. You have ended the addiction of _____ once and for all. It will not rise up again, in the Name of Jesus Christ.
- I think God's thoughts. (Philippians 4:8)
- I am happy and I am righteous. (2 Corinthians 5:21)
- I am blessed. I am prosperous. I am rich. I am free. I have a sound mind. (2 Timothy 1:7)
- I can now fulfill God's purpose for my life because I am **FREE**!
- I meditate day and night on God's Word and God's goodness for my life. I see myself successful, prosperous, and **FREE**!
- I am a new creature in Christ. I am not ashamed of how the devil used me. I'm not ashamed of my past. **JESUS TOOK MY SHAME!** Now, I can help others be free from shame.
- Instead of your shame, there shall be a double portion; instead of dishonor, they shall rejoice in their lot; therefore, in their land they shall possess a double portion; they shall have everlasting joy. I have a double portion. I have everlasting **JOY**! (Isaiah 61:7)
- God is restoring everything to me that the devil stole: my health, my wealth, my self-respect, my dignity, my righteousness, my virginity, my joy, my businesses, my houses, my family, my children, my spouse, my careers, my purpose, my beauty, my youth, my money, and my self-love!
- **RESTORE! RESTORE! RESTORE!** (Isaiah 42:22) **I SAY RESTORE!**
- I have the peace of God which passeth all understanding. I am delivered! (Philippians 4:7)

AFFIRMATIONS

If you were like me and no one ever affirmed you, I want to affirm you today!

- God created you, and **YOU** are *VERY GOOD!* (Genesis 1:31)
- God made you, and **YOU** are **SOOO** beautiful! (Ecclesiastes 3:11)
- God has delivered you, and **YOU** are righteous! (Genesis 15:6)
- God will increase **YOU** more and more! (Psalm 115:14)
- Get your eyes *OFF* of your past and look to your future! Your future is *SO BRIGHT!* (Jeremiah 29:11)
- **YOU** are fearfully- and wonderfully-made. You can do *ALL* things with Jesus' help! (Psalm 139:14)
- The **GREATER ONE** lives in you, and you are a force to be reckoned with! (1 John 4:4)
- God shows you **EXTRAVAGANT FAVOR!** (Psalm 112:1, Amplified)
- You are more than able to do all God's predestined you to do, to give, and to be! Just **BE**! (2 Corinthians 9:8)
- You have special gifts and talents! (Matthew 25:14-15)
- You are a creative being. No one creates like you do! You are made in the image of God and He is **THE CREATOR!**
- You are **ONE OF A KIND!** No one else has your finger print! You are extremely **SPECIAL!** (Deuteronomy 7:6)
- You are 1,000 times more than you are. (Deuteronomy 1:11) So, whatever you think you are, you're 1,000 times more!
- You are God's special creation! You are the apple of His eye! (Deuteronomy 32:10)

Who'd A Thought Deliverance Would Come?

- God's plans for you are for good and not evil, to give you an expected end. **EXPECT BIG THINGS!** (Jeremiah 29:11)
- God is so pleased with you! **NOTHING** can stop God's plan for your life!
- **GOD REALLY LOVES YOU!** (John 3:16)

MY ANCHOR SCRIPTURE

As you read your Bible daily, you will find scriptures that stand out to you. You will want to jot them down and confess them daily as well!

Below is the scripture I memorized and confessed regularly upon my initial deliverance - the scripture I term "My Anchor Scripture":

> *"Fear thou not; for I am with thee: be not dismayed; for I am thy God: I will strengthen thee; yea, I will help thee; yea, I will uphold thee with the right hand of my righteousness."*
> (Isaiah 41:10)

Now, **PERSONALIZE** that scripture.

"Thank you, Lord: I am free! Thank you that I fear not. Thank you that you are with me. Thank you that I am not dismayed any longer, for you are my God. Thank you for strengthening me. Thank you for helping me. Thank you for upholding me. Thank you for setting me free and making me righteous."

I'm *ALL* that...because **DELIVERANCE HAS COME!**

Now, continue to maintain a steady diet of the Word and keep it coming out of your mouth! It is your sword that you fight with supernaturally!

REMEMBER: Deliverance comes when **YOU** decide **YOU** want to step over into that place of freedom that awaits you. It is the next blank page of a new chapter in your life, waiting to be fulfilled with what you want to create and write on it!

ABOUT THE AUTHOR

Dr. Lucy A. Todd is a devoted Christ-follower, a loving mother, an active member of civic organizations, and she enjoys boating and frequenting museums. She is a Business Consultant, Personal Life Coach, Member of Delta Mu Delta, an Author, and Speaker with works spanning the Christian sector and business arenas.

She is an accomplished business woman and holds a Doctorate from Capella University with specializations in Strategy and Innovation - a graduate with distinction.

Dr. Lucy A. Todd

Dr. Todd's exceptional business acumen is undergirded by her faith in God. Dr. Todd is an avid learner and continues to stay abreast of the latest advances in innovation and technology, delivering added value to her clients with a burning passion for their success. More importantly, she remains in a constant state of renewing her mind.

Dr. Todd loves Jesus Christ, and one of her goals is to share with the world His immense love and His ongoing deliverance-readiness. Regardless of what has transpired in people's lives, God wants them set free.

Additionally, Dr. Todd enjoys inspiring and enlightening others, utilizing the gifts and talents God has given her - doing so on a level the world is not familiar with, all while glorifying God.

Learn more about Dr. Todd by visiting:

www.ToddExpertConsulting.com

www.PearlyGatesPublishing.com

For Speaking Engagements, contact her via email at:

DrLucyT1@gmail.com

Bibliography

Allen, J. (1960). *As a Man Thinketh*. Peter Pauper Press, Inc. White Plains, NY.

Breathnach, S. (1995). *Simple Abundance: A Daybook of Comfort and Joy*. Warner Books, Time Warner Book Group, New York, NY.

Collins, J. (2001). *Why Some Companies Make the Leap...and Others Don't. Good to Great*. HarperCollins Publishers, Inc, New York, NY.

Copeland, K. (2011). *The Blessing of the Lord Makes Rich and He Adds No Sorrow with It*. Kenneth Copeland Publications, Fort Worth, TX.

Covey, S. (1989). *The 7 Habits of Highly Effective People*. Simon and Schuster, New York, NY.

Dollar, C. (2008). *8 Steps to Create the Life You Want: The Anatomy of a Successful Life*. Time Warner Trade Publishing, New York, NY.

Facing Addiction in America. (n.d.). *Chapter 1: Introduction and Overview of the Report*. The Surgeon General's Report on Alcohol, Drugs and Health. Retrieved 12 March 2017 from https://addiction.surgeongeneral.gov/chapter-1-introduction.pdf.

Golos, V. (2011). *Vocabulary of Silence*. Red Hen Press, Los Angeles, CA.

Harvey, S. (2014). *Act Like a Success, Think Like a Success: Discovering Your Gift and the Way to Life's Riches*. HarperCollins Publishers, New York, NY.

Leaf, C. Dr. (2015). *Switch on Your Brain*. Baker Publishing Group, Grand Rapids, MI.

Leaf, C. Dr. (2016). *A Neuroscientific Approach to a Sharper Mind and Healthier Life*. Think & Eat Yourself Smart. Baker Publishing Group, Grand Rapids, MI.

Meyer, J. (1995). *Battlefield of the Mind*. Time Warner Book Group, New York, NY.

Nichols, L. (2009). *No Matter What! 9 Steps to Living the Life You Love - Grand Central Life & Style.* Hachette Book Group, New York, NY.

Osteen, J. (2013). *Break Out! 5 Keys to Go Beyond Your Barriers and Live an Extraordinary Life: Faith Words.* Hachette Book Group, New York, NY.

Oyedepo, D. (2006). *Commanding the Supernatural.* Dominion Publishing House, Ogun State, Nigeria.

Quinn, R.W. and Quinn, R.E. (2015). *Lift: The Fundamental State of Leadership.* Berrett-Koehler Publishers, Inc., Oakland, CA.

Roberts, O. (2002). *When You See the Invisible, You Can Do the Impossible.* Still Doing the Impossible. Destiny Image Publishers, Inc., Shippensburg, PA.

Safrai, Z. (1996). *Gergesa, Gerasa, or Gadara? Where Did Jesus' Miracle Occur?* Retrieved 12 March 2017 from http://www.jerusalemperspective.com/2771/

Virtue, D. (2015). *Angel Therapy.* Retrieved 12 March 2017 from http://www.angeltherapy.com/blog/what-meaning-number-12.

Williamson, M. (1996). *A Return to Love: Reflections on the Principles of "A Course in Miracles".* HarperCollins Publishers, New York, NY.

www.ingramcontent.com/pod-product-compliance
Lightning Source LLC
Chambersburg PA
CBHW060525100426
42743CB00009B/1432